TIME AMONG THE NAVAJO

TIME AMONG THE NAVAJO

Traditional Lifeways on the Reservation

By Kathy Eckles Hooker

Photographs by Helen Lau Running

Foreword by Danny K. Blackgoat

Museum of New Mexico Press

to my husband, Bill
to my children, Megan and Sara
and to my friends Kay and Irene

K. E. H.

The Museum of New Mexico Press is a unit of the Museum of New Mexico, a division of the State Office of Cultural Affairs.

Library-of-Congress Catalog Card Number: 90–63711
ISBN: 0-89013-221-6

Manufactured in the United States of America
Project editor: Mary Wachs
Design by GLYPHICS / Terry Duffy Design
Illustrations by Sally Blakemore

Museum of New Mexico Press
P.O. Box 2087
Santa Fe, NM 87504–2087

CONTENTS

FOREWORD

I am a Navajo and I belong to the earth. The earth is my mother, my provider, and my caretaker. I am her child. She nourishes me from her body and her soul.

I belong to the land. I am rooted in my mother earth. Her deserts, canyons, and mesas encircle me. Her mountains, fields, and forests are a part of me. I am one with nature, and she is one with me.

I belong to my people, the *Diné*, meaning The People. Our clans live between the four sacred mountains. These mountains protect us. On this land between these mountains we strive for unity and balance. When all is in balance with our Earth Mother, our Sky Father, and The People, then there is *hozho*, or harmony.

Time Among the Navajo is about my people, the Navajos. We are the earth-walkers who survive from the land. We are truly the people of the earth. We are wise and know the way to be. This book tells how my people live and how we use the gifts and blessings from our mother, the earth.

Danny K. Blackgoat
Flagstaff, Arizona

ACKNOWLEDGMENTS

When I first began the research for this book, I knew little of Navajo tradition and lifeways. Even though I was an outsider, The People shared parts of their world with patience and kindness.

Navajo Danny Blackgoat gave much to this project. He wrote the Foreword and arranged many meetings with his mother, Roberta. Sally Worker asked her parents, Stella and Sam, if I could visit in their home. The Deal family introduced me to Hazel Nez, Mary Joe Yazzie, and Oskar Whitehair. Manuel Shirley from Dilcon, Arizona, brought me to the home of Yazzie and his mother, Addie. Alice Spencer contacted her mother-in-law, Mary, for me. Steve Darden, the first Navajo to serve on the Flagstaff City Council, read an earlier version of the manuscript and offered words about mother earth and father sky. Without these people, this project would not have been possible.

My husband Bill and daughter Megan were patient as I wrote and rewrote this book. I thank them for their tolerance and support. I do not know who among us was happiest to have it completed.

Helen, my partner and photographer, accompanied me on all excursions. Sometimes we had to leave at 3:00 in the morning. Helen was awake, packed and ready to go. When we began this project, I was anxious. Helen was reassuring and full of encouragement.

Many others helped with this work. I would like to mention a select few by name. Ann Rice, Lois Raney, and Barbara Twitchell encouraged me to begin writing. Paul Tissler, Ellen Allen, Tim Varner, Nancy Bene, Ursula Wallentine-Flores, Frances Short, Letty David, Lois Thompson, Jan Koons, Pam Young-Wolff, Linda Besnette, Judy Yescalis, Ann Kramer, and Mary Beth Green shared their knowledge, materials, and support. Bob Koons helped to obtain a grant so that the project could be completed. Bud Greenlee assisted me in understanding my motivation behind the book. LuLu Santa-Maria believed in this project and helped with its marketing. And David Young-Wolff processed many of the photographs.

The one person who most helped me to understand the true meaning of this work was my editor, Jean Zukowski-Faust. She spent hours with me as I wrote and rewrote. Our best working times were in the evenings. I would arrive at her home at 9:00 and would not leave until 1:00 or 2:00 in the morning. Jean understood even better than I my love for the Navajo people and allowed me to discover this on my own. Her support, encouragement, and, most importantly, her honesty enabled me to create this book.

To Jean and to the others, I thank you.

The earth being
our mother is a
beautiful
mother—giving
us life, nurturing
us daily, and
continuing to
sustain life
for us. She is
beautiful;
therefore, we
are as beautiful
as she.

Steven A. Darden

THE BEGINNING

When I lived on the Navajo Reservation beginning in the late 1970s and taught at a local boarding school, I spent much of my free time riding throughout the countryside around Dilcon, Arizona, slowly passing through the Navajo settlements where my students lived. With a curiosity that must have at times bordered on nosiness, I stared intently into the camps and studied the hogans, summer shelters, and corrals. On lucky days I saw young children playing or women weaving. I longed to be invited into the lives of these people, to lessen the distance between us.

Once a rapport was established with my Navajo students, I talked with them about their home life, asking: "How do you live?" "What do your homes look like?" "What kind of foods do you eat?" Once I asked a student what he had done over the weekend. He said, "I hunted prairie dogs, cooked them, and ate them." To him it was a report of an ordinary sequence; to me it was a surprise.

At first I was astonished by the Navajos' close relationship with the earth and by their capacity both to exist within the monoculture of dominant American society and yet to hold on to their traditional ways. I was most strongly drawn to those for whom maintaining a traditional life was not a choice but rather the continuation of practices that were part of an implicit heritage. This minority culture keeping to its ancestral ways exists as something of an endangered species within the dominant society. And yet, for many Navajo these traditions are ineluctable.

My students were asked to make a list of all the traditional Navajo tasks practiced by their families. The final list included activities such as building a hogan, making yucca shampoo, hauling water, cooking Navajo blood cakes, and grinding corn. The students were amused at their teacher's lack of knowledge about their lifestyle, so for the next month, these young people dictated oral histories covering the specifics of Navajo traditions, which I recorded in book form and presented to them at the end of the school year.

This glimpse into Navajo lifeways impelled me further in the desire to know what it is to live as a traditional Navajo on the reservation. Helen and I began by making contacts with Navajos throughout the Western Reservation. We found many who were willing to teach us their "old ways." Setting up the visits was hit-and-miss. I would talk to one Navajo friend who might know of another who could show us how to make a bé'éžó (grass brush). In turn, the woman who made the brush might know of someone who would be willing to make pottery for us or another who would weave a rug. Because these Navajos had no telephone and collected their mail from a trading post once every two weeks, communication between us was neither swift nor sure. We sent letters and hoped they were received.

Our first visits were awkward. Helen and I were strangers, though expected. Our apprehension at being turned away was real and, we learned, needless.

One fall afternoon, Helen and I drove to Sam and Stella Worker's camp, where Sam was to make a pair of moccasins. Above their small hogan the deep-blue sky and, in the background, the snow-covered San Francisco Peaks to the north offered a spectacular view. All seemed still at the camp, but as we walked toward the hogan we could hear the thump, thump, thumping of Stella's weaving tools tapping yarn into a rug. We knocked at the door, heard a faint "Come in," and entered. Stella, a plump woman in her sixties, sat cross-legged at the loom. Sam was nearby, sorting through his moccasin-making tools. The first utterance Stella made was, "I am sorry we don't have a nice place to live like white people." My mind went blank. How could I respond to such a statement without seeming patronizing? Ironically, Helen and I had just commented to ourselves about how lovely the Worker hogan appeared with the mountain peaks in the background. From my heart, surmounting the uneasiness, I responded, "It is beautiful here."

In the next moment we found ourselves drawing closer to Stella and the rug she was weaving. The loom held a stunning example of the weaving for which she is renowned throughout the reservation. Turning her head slightly, she introduced herself with a soft handshake and a nod. Sam, who speaks no English, greeted us the same way. Slowly we began to relax as Sam sat down on the floor of his one-room home, smoothed out a cowhide, and without comment began to make a pair of moccasins.

Somewhat by accident, Sam and Stella became our true friends. Helen's camera broke twice during our initial visits. In all, Sam sewed three pairs of moc-

casins for us. We learned in the meantime that Stella makes bé'éžós and Navajo tea, so we established the basis for frequent return visits and the opportunity to share more of our lives and theirs.

We learned from the Workers a great deal about their concerns for keeping their land in view of the relocation of Navajos and Hopis from territory caught in the Hopi-Navajo Land Dispute.

Both Sam Worker and all of his children were born on the land the family occupied. The thought of losing their home made Stella heartsick. She held on to the hope that because her son had served with the army during the Vietnam War that she and Sam would be able to stay; unfortunately, that was not to be the case. Sam and Stella Worker moved the following year into a prefabricated house about ten miles from their land. Their hogan and animal shelters were destroyed. Today, the Workers seem out of place in their three-bedroom, carpeted house.

We heard many stories about the land dispute. Besides Sam and Stella Worker, many of the other contributors to the project were required by law to leave their land. Ella and Leonard Deal were more fortunate than some. The Deals live on the border of the disputed area and consequently have lost only a small portion of land—that which located their outhouse.

Ella is a tall, slender grandmother who has lived near the Hard Rocks area all her life. Leonard is a short man with a rugged face, weathered from the dry Arizona climate. The Deals maintain the seminomadic existence typical of traditional Navajos and are known for the garden they tend in a valley close to their summer camp. Ella plants a large garden each spring. This year, Helen and I will watch everything mature through the summer and on into the harvest.

Ella and I tromp through the potato fields one summer afternoon. She and her daughters have planted an acre, and each row stands straight and neat. I kneel down to examine one of the plants, noticing a delicate pink flower. Knowing little about gardening, I innocently ask Ella how the plants are able to remain standing with the potatoes growing from the flowers. My ignorance stimulates a long, educational conversation about farming. We sit on kitchen chairs outside in the warm afternoon in the shade of the large cottonwood tree in front of Ella's hogan. The Navajo process of planting is similar to the Anglo way; however, the uniqueness of Ella's planting style is to plant with a rhythm and to care for each plant individually. "We bring a can of water to each plant to make sure it grows." Her voice becomes softer as she talks about the Navajo way of giving and taking care of one another. "Gardens are for feeding the family and for giving to others who are hungry. We help everyone because we all come from our earth."

The close ties among The People and within the Deal family were easy to see on the day the Deals branded their cattle. Their grown children came home to help, and each person was assigned a specific task for the day. It was August, and grandchildren and grandparents alike worked many hours in the unrelenting dust and heat. At the end of the workday, they sat eating the evening meal and talking quietly, sharing the experiences of the day. Our lack of understanding of Navajo perhaps was felt most disappointingly that day.

Oskar Whitehair is a good friend of Ella and Leonard Deal. He lives in a pink cinder-block house in Cactus Valley, Arizona, on the Navajo Reservation. We have been led here by Ella Deal to see the large, intricately woven corral that Oskar has built. The trip to Cactus Valley has taken us up over winding roads, up mountainsides, and close to canyon walls. We are grateful to our guide. After greeting us, Oskar sets out for his fields to bring in the sheep for the evening.

With the sheep locked in the corral for the night, Oskar's mood changed. He became serious as he talked about the federal order that bid him to move from his land. The land-dispute issue had him deeply troubled. In September of 1982 Oskar organized a conference at his camp and invited many Navajo and Anglo officials to discuss the situation. Oskar made it clear at the conference that he was not moving. What he said at that time touched many.

When it was time for us to leave, we bade Oskar goodbye. He shook our hands and said, "Now I hope you understand our problem." As of this writing he still lives in Cactus Valley.

Ella Deal acted as liaison for many of our Navajo contacts. Her sister, Hazel K. Nez, lived about two miles from Ella's land. We visited her numerous times.

The first several were awkward due to a tactical error I'd made in our first visit. I'd made the mistake of asking Hazel if she would share the way she had learned to weave. To me, it was a natural question, but Hazel stared back with anger in her eyes. I realized too late that I had forgotten the Navajo way, which is to move slowly among The People so that trust can be established. In our next few visits, Hazel was quiet. Although her angered look was gone, she would only respond when asked a direct question.

One wintry evening, as she sat at the loom in her weaving shed, Hazel began speaking of her thirteen grown children and her husband, whom she referred to as "the old man." He had passed away a few years earlier, and though her children came to visit her often, it was obvious Hazel was still grieving. From a shaky beginning, our relationship grew.

Hazel's home is about twenty miles from the Black Mesa Trading Post, a drive mostly on dirt roads. On the cold morning of our last scheduled visit, about eight inches of snow had fallen. We had had an understanding that snow would be the one factor that might keep us from a scheduled visit. However, I was so anxious to see the completed rug that we fought the dangerous road conditions to her home. When Helen and I arrived around 11:00 that morning, Hazel came out, giggling and looking embarrassed. "Oh, no! You are here! I cannot believe it! I thought you wouldn't come because of the snow. I have lots to do on the rug." We entered her weaving shed to find only a few uncompleted inches. We estimated only a few additional hours at the most.

Hazel immediately sat down and began to weave. Her legs were crossed and her back and shoulders were rounded as she picked up her weaving tools and yarn. She remained in this position hour after hour, never taking a break. Finally, eight hours later, Hazel had completed her rug. She stood up slowly, complaining of stiff legs, yet her face radiated a big smile.

She carried the rug into her home and placed it across her bed. With a brush, she moved the bristles back and forth to clean the rug thoroughly. She folded it neatly and handed it to me. I gave her eight fifty-dollar bills. She took the money and said, "I weave today. I eat tonight."

A friend of Hazel's is Roberta Blackgoat, one of the first to share her lifestyle with us. A hard worker, she lives alone in Big Mountain, Arizona, on land that she believes is a part of her. She, too, has been ordered off her land. Roberta's days are spent chopping wood, hauling water, weaving, herding sheep, and grinding corn.

She has a motherly concern for her animals. One chilly spring night, Roberta was worried about the sheep she had sheared, fearful the animals would be cold. Not able to sleep, she arose at 3:00 in the morning to put a burlap bag around each animal for warmth. "I put sweaters on them," she explained.

In all the tasks she performs, there is perfectionism. Woodpiles are neatly stacked; rugs are tightly woven with fine symmetrical designs; blood cakes are perfect; cornmeal is finely ground to a light powder.

Although her house appears cluttered, each item has a designated place. At night, Helen and I sleep next to Roberta. We have brought sleeping bags; she crawls into a pile of seven or eight blankets piled on top of one another. In the morning, she neatly folds each blanket and places them on a shelf.

Roberta loves her way of life to the degree that she is willing to fight for it. She is fighting the relocation by whatever means short of violence that are possible. She has visited Washington, D.C., appealing to government officials. She has appeared on radio and television to tell her story. She steadfastly refuses to move.

Roberta's son Danny fights alongside his mother. Danny left the reservation for a number of years, but found his life to be confusing. Like many young Navajo men, he discovered that it is difficult to live in two worlds. After a troubled period, he knew he must return to the land and the Navajo way.

Danny was comfortably at home as he chopped wood for Roberta one March afternoon. He swung the ax in a wide arc, loaded the wood into the truck, and drove to his mother's camp. Next, he traveled to a nearby well to fill his mother's water barrels. It was evident Danny enjoyed helping Roberta. His soft voice was firm and proud, for life was not confusing when he was home on the land.

Mary Spencer, who lives in the southwest portion of the reservation, not far from Winslow, speaks no English and uses her son, Bruce, who lives in Dilcon, as a translator. Like many Navajos, Mary, a widow, has lived on the land her entire life. The tribe recently built her a new hogan with a tile floor and drywall panels, and even though Mary enjoys the comforts of her modern hogan, she still lives the traditional Navajo way.

Our first experience with muddy Navajo roads, an inescapable feature of wintertime on the reservation, occurred on our way to Mary's. With only the eight miles of dirt road from the highway to go, we thought our trip nearly over. But snow from a storm earlier in the week had left the road so muddy that the Jeep seemed to be moving sideways rather than straight ahead. At one point, I was sure we were going to slide into a ten-foot-deep ditch. It was then that Helen offered the wise suggestion that we "just keep moving and do not stop." Eventually we slid into Mary's camp.

We had come to learn how to make yucca shampoo. Mary assumed her role as teacher and lectured directly to us in Navajo. We turned to Bruce and Alice for translation, and Alice nervously took the cue, uneasy that she might not be correctly relaying Mary's words.

Another of our contacts was Mary Joe Yazzie, a single parent in her forties who works for Peabody Coal on the night shift and makes pots with whatever spare time she has. We traveled with Mary Joe to a pit near her home to dig for clay. For the second ingredient we visited a piñon forest to gather pitch. Our luck this day is good; says Mary Joe, "I can't believe it! Sometimes we would come to the piñon trees and look all day and find nothing!"

The clay-digging pit is close to the home of Mary Joe's mother-in-law, Annette, who is also a fine potter. It is decided that the pot-making will take place here. The vessel is built by hand and left to dry in Annette's hogan. We arrange to meet five days later for the firing.

With some of our contacts we spend just a short time, as with Joe Gordy who showed us how he makes a horse hobble.

Another friend, Yazzie, a soft-spoken young man in his twenties who lives traditionally, is knowledgeable about materials for building hogans and summer shelters. He took us to see his mother's mud oven. Addie Yazzie is an elegant woman who speaks no English but would smile, giggle, and nod as we talked with her son.

Besides her mud oven, Addie was proud of her hogan, pointing to the ceiling construction made of juniper wood and formed of logs in a circular, spiraling design. Her hogan was twenty-five years old. She knew it would last.

When we first met, Delbert Begay was in the process of building a hogan for his mother. This contact was important to us, as partially built hogans are difficult to find. Initially, we were led to believe that Delbert spoke no English. We asked questions and he stared back. One of his children offered translation. In this way, Delbert listed in Navajo the materials necessary to build a hogan and the process involved in constructing one.

A few weeks later at a nearby trading post, Helen and I heard a man call out to us, "Hi! Hi! How are you?" In clear English, Delbert asked how our project was going. We spoke together for about twenty minutes. We were delighted that somehow we had proved ourselves to Delbert and had been accepted.

At the project's end, I saw a common thread: Each topic in some way related to the land. They easily fell into five categories: plants, water, wood, animals, and soil. Stella Worker's Navajo tea and *bé'ézǒ*, Roberta Blackgoat's corn grinding, Lavern Tsosie's kneel-down bread, and Mary Spencer's yucca shampoo all come from plants on the Navajo Reservation. Danny Blackgoat and the Deal family show the uses of water, Danny hauling it for drinking and the Deals watering their garden. Danny's chopping of firewood, Yazzie's summer shelter, and Oskar Whitehair's corral used the resource of wood. From the animals come Joe Gordy's horse hobble, Hazel Nez's Navajo rug, Roberta Blackgoat's Navajo blood cake, the Deals' family cattle branding, and Sam Worker's moccasins. The earth itself is found in Addie Yazzie's mud oven, Delbert Begay's hogan, and Mary Joe Yazzie's pottery.

As Danny Blackgoat noted, "With the sky above, we Navajos are the walkers of the earth and are one with it."

▾▾▾▾▾

Plants are one
offspring of the
Earth Mother
and Sky Father.
Utilized to
perpetuate life,
they are
symbolic of the
essence of life.

Steven A. Darden

YUCCA SHAMPOO

Mary Spencer plans to wash her granddaughter Lisa's hair in the Navajo way, using yucca from her land. Mary, her son Bruce, his wife Alice, and Lisa drive into the hills close to Mary's camp to find a fresh yucca. "Old yucca is just no good," Bruce says. "It sure gets rotten. New ones are the best and make good soap, and I'm sure there is one around here." We find a young yucca within moments.

Shovel in hand, Bruce carefully digs up the soft soil around the plant. With one tug, he pulls out the yucca, exposing its muddy root. Holding the plant in place on the ground, he chops the root off with his shovel blade. As Alice and Lisa return the plant to the soil, Bruce shovels dirt around it, explaining, "We always give the yucca back to the land."

Mary cleans the mud from the root by rubbing it briskly on some nearby damp grass. Over and over, she wipes the root until it is only a small stick with bark. From the size of the root the women decide they have enough for one washing. We return to camp, leaving land that looks as if it has never been touched.

Bruce begins the soap-making process by cracking the root with a hammer to break the bark-covering shell. As he removes the shell, a white root emerges that is fibrous, slick, and soapy. While a large pan of water warms, Mary emphasizes that "the pan and your hands have to be clean, not greasy, or the yucca won't work—it won't make soap." The results, it is clear, will be worth the effort. "I've used yucca on my hair all of my life, and I like the way it works."

In a large metal bowl, Mary splashes water over the clean root, producing a thick, white lather. Mary rubs the root as if it is a bar of soap, and gentle bubbles begin to form. As the bubbles change into thick suds, Mary continues the rubbing. After a few minutes, the bowl overflows with lather.

Lisa unties her long, black ponytail, bends over, and lowers her hair into the lather. Her grandmother scoops up the sudsy water and washes it into Lisa's hair. Mary massages her granddaughter's scalp, working the yucca suds gently through the black strands. Lisa says she loves the soft rubbing of her grandmother's hands on her head; also hearing the swishing of water and the quiet popping of the white bubbles around her ears. After a few minutes, Mary tells Lisa that her hair is clean. It is time to rinse.

Alice hands another pot of warm water to Mary, who slowly pours it over Lisa's soapy head. The rinsing takes several minutes, but soon the girl's wet hair shines. Alice squeezes her daughter's hair with a towel, and when she removes the wrapping, Lisa throws her head back so that her long hair first flies up into the air

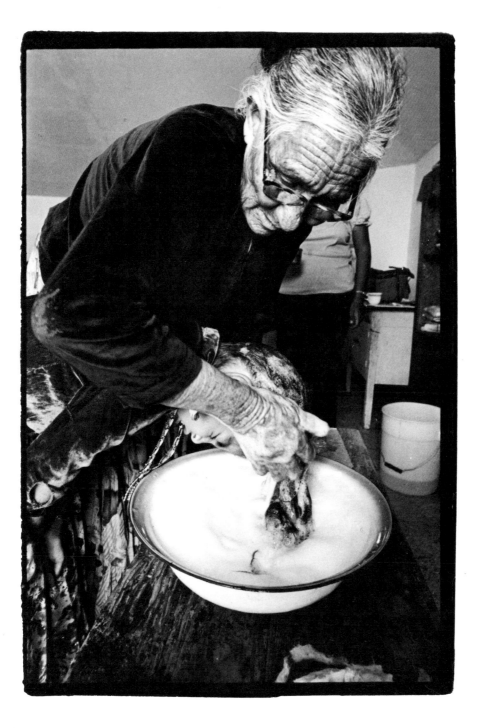

and then flops down on her back. The few yucca fibers sticking to the strands of hair drop to the floor as Lisa shakes her head from side to side, bouncing her hair in a hair-drying dance. She moves close to the fire to allow its warmth to reach her hair.

"That soap from the store gives you dandruff. This yucca doesn't," Mary explains. "It makes hair nice. Some people can get a rash from it, but most Navajos don't. Yucca makes hair shiny, and it makes hair grow longer."

To finish the hairdressing tasks, Mary Spencer brings out a brush called a *bé'ézó*, carefully removing it from the bag in which it is stored. The *bé'ézó* is a bundle of stiff, dried perennial grass (called "Sandhill" muhly) that grows near sandy areas. "We pick the grass in August and September after it has been dried by the hot summer sun," explains Alice. Mary takes the *bé'ézó* and lightly hits the ends against the palm of her hand. Over and over, she taps the grass ends to make them even.

Lisa kneels close to her grandmother as Mary combs the now-dry hair first with her fingers. Cradling the hair in her hand, she begins brushing; the *bé'ézó* makes scratching sounds against Lisa's head. Soon her long hair becomes straight and glossy.

The final step is the Navajo hair bundle. Mary pulls Lisa's hair back over her shoulders, takes a hank of white yarn, and wraps it once around the hair to make an ordinary ponytail. Next, the ponytail is folded three times until it reaches the scalp to form a long double loop. She wraps the yarn tightly around the center of the loop of hair, then fans out the hair above and below the tie to form two full bundles. Mary looks at Lisa with approval. They are ready to be photographed.

Mary Spencer has put on her turquoise and silver jewelry. She has tied her hair in a Navajo bundle. Grandmother and granddaughter sit side by side. Mary Spencer's face has the beauty of age and experience. Lisa's is young and attentive. She now has the knowledge of the yucca and will one day teach her children how to use it.

THE *BÉ'ÉŽÓ* (GRASS BRUSH)

Stella Worker takes pride in showing the tools she makes, such as her *bé'éžó*, which she makes every fall. "It's the best time of year," she explains. "The cool weather makes the stems hard and good for brushing, cooking, and cleaning."

Navajo women pick the grass for their brushes in bunches and bind it together with string, cloth, or yucca leaves. Once bound, the *bé'éžó* is one foot to two feet in length and one inch to two inches in diameter. The sweeping end of the brush is coarse while the other end is full and bushy.

One clear October day, Stella and I hike over the hill by her hogan to a *bé'éžó* picking place, a meadow full of sage and muhly. Once there, she sits down with legs sideways, spreads out her skirt, and picks a *bé'éžó* bundle. Her fingers break the culm close to the ground and pull each sheath away. She puts the clean stem stalks on her skirt. At one point, she stops and lets me feel the stiff end of the grass. "You see, it makes a pretty good brush." Stella resumes her picking and cleaning until her skirt is full. She scoops up the grass with one hand and taps the ends against her palm to make them even. "I am almost finished. All I need to do is tie the grass together."

Close to the muhly is a dying yucca plant that easily yields its leaves. Stella chooses a long, thin leaf and ties it a few inches up from the base of the brush. "Sometimes I use cloth or a rubber band to keep the grass together, but I think the yucca leaf does the best job." Stella binds the grass tightly and looks at the loose leaves that hang from the brush top. "Now all I have to do is clean off the *bé'éžó* by sweeping it across a nearby plant." With a quick, sure motion, she brushes the *bé'éžó* over a thorny bush and the leafy part falls to the ground. Stella holds up the brush and exclaims: "Look! I have a nice fat one! I'll take you back and show you what this can do."

Back in her hogan, Stella is eager to begin her *bé'éžó* demonstration. Holding the *bé'éžó* as if she is presenting it to me, she says, "It is good for dusting. We take the soft end and flick it on the dust. See, like this." Stella rapidly brushes the dust from her table, saying, "It does the job!"

The brush is also useful in cooking. "You can use it as a spoon to stir the cornmeal, and you can use it as a broom to sweep your stones after grinding the corn." She strokes the coarse brush over her metate and its stems scrape the stone clean. "It also makes a good sieve. We use juniper ash water when we make cornmeal patties. The brush is spread apart and keeps the juniper ash in and lets the juniper water through."

Admiring her newly made *bé'éžó*, Stella reflects on the tradition of their making. "You know, I make these brushes for many years. My mom would herd sheep and we would bring these brushes home. A long time ago, when there were no white people's stores, this kind of brush is what all The People used. This is the old-fashioned Navajo way. I still use these brushes today because they work really, really well."

GRINDING CORN

Helen and I arrange a visit with Roberta Blackgoat to watch her collect two life essentials — water and wood. When visiting a Navajo, there is a settling-in period before a productive meeting can begin. After first strolling around Roberta's camp, we are then invited into her rockhouse. We sit in the enveloping silence. There are occasional words when we ask about her grown children or when we speak about the snow falling outside. Then it is silent again. To our relief, Roberta suddenly decides it is time to make cornmeal patties because she feels hungry for them.

Making cornmeal patties is a time-consuming task and so Roberta carefully arranges the ingredients in an organized fashion. First, she lines up all of her cooking tools: goat hide, metate, mano, and brick. The metate and mano are traditional stones which Roberta uses for grinding. Both are smooth and rounded; the metate is large and rectangular, while the mano is smaller and oblong. "You can make patties with corn that has been ground once, but I want this cornmeal to be as fine as possible, so I regrind again and it becomes better." Roberta turns toward her kitchen shelf, takes a canning jar full of ground lavender-blue cornmeal, and places it close to the stones.

Every part of the process appears easy and natural. Roberta spreads the goat hide on the floor, with the fur side down. Under the goat skin lies the brick to raise one end of the metate. Roberta positions the metate carefully so that no sound is made when it touches the goat hide. She then sets the mano in the metate's concave area for stability. The metate is the base and the mano the grinder. Held firmly in two hands, the mano is pushed back and pulled forward over the corn kernels on the metate. Roberta and the two stones embody the act of corn grinding in terms of rhythm and movement: the slow, graceful blending of purpose and motion flow with an earth energy I have never observed before.

This metate and mano have been in her family for many years. "I have these stones a long time. These were my uncle's. He made them. He grew lots of corn. After he died, they went to my aunt. Then she got too old for them and didn't grind corn anymore. She gave them to me thirty years ago when my son Danny was little." Roberta adds, "I started to grind the corns when I was six. My aunts thought I ought to be a corn grinder and to learn this grinding way. They used to hide me in the small hogan. They wanted me to hide and grind all day long, but the policeman would come and look for me. He said I was supposed to be in school." Roberta liked school — but she also liked being "good with the corns."

As Roberta works, fine cornmeal drops slowly, steadily building a lavender mound at the base of the stone. When she finishes, the entire jar of blue cornmeal has been reground. The pile sits high on the goat skin. With a *bé'ézó*, she sweeps the remaining ground meal onto the mound. The hide glistens with the rich lavender-blue color. Roberta scoops up the meal with her hands, drops it into a white bowl, and then sits back on her heels to rest.

"There is lots you can do with this meal. I can put syrup or sugar in it and make a sweet tamale corn pancake; I can add hot water to make cornmeal soup or make flat pancakes and fry them; or I can mix fat and boiling water, then drop in cornmeal and stir. It makes a good, lumpy soup. Sometimes I mix mutton, water, and cornmeal," Roberta explains proudly.

For fifty-five years, Roberta has been making cornmeal. She loves the grinding of the corn and the scraping sounds of the stones as she continues a Navajo tradition.

CORNMEAL PATTIES

Evening sets in, obscuring the falling snow. The wind is blowing fiercely, but inside the rockhouse a warm fire crackles in Roberta's woodburning stove. She tells us we look hungry for dinner, so she begins to gather the ingredients for cornmeal patties: the cornmeal she reground this afternoon, a pan of hot water, and a bowl of saltwater. Roberta picks up a shovel and goes outside to a fire pit, where she lifts the snow from the ashes and extracts a clump of juniper ash. All the while, the snow swirls around her as we watch from the window. When she returns, snowflakes cling to her hair, face, and clothing. They melt quickly, though, in the warmth of her hogan. Roberta places the ashes on her stove to warm and says, "I'll mix this ash with the blue cornmeal because it is important for my patties. It helps to keep the patties' blue color and to make them get big." Juniper ash is her leavening.

Roberta scoops two handfuls of blue cornmeal into another white mixing bowl. With her finger, she neatly taps a small pit in the center of the cornmeal mound and fills it with a small amount of the juniper ash. Using the stick side of a *bé'éžó* as a spoon, she stirs the cornmeal and ash. She explains, "Now I'll mix the leftover ash with hot, hot water. I call this ash soup. I'll pour the clean ash water into the bowl. I use my *bé'éžó*

as a sieve to pour the clean ash water through. When this mixture gets kind of cold, I'll make the food."

She then mixes the dough, tests it, and says, "It feels a little too soft. I'll have to add more cornmeal. . . . Now it is okay." Her mixture resembles lavender clay. She takes a fist-sized ball of dough, squeezes it between her palms, and forms a thick patty. After her moistened fingertips have rounded the edges of the patty, it is ready for the hot, oiled skillet. "In the old days, my family used a rock to cook on over the fire. I used to have one, but it broke, so now I use the skillet."

Roberta shapes the remaining cornmeal patties; soon the skillet holds five cakes. After browning them on both sides, she puts them in the oven for fifteen minutes to cook all the way through; then she removes them to cool and dips them into saltwater, explaining that the salty flavor enhances the taste. Holding a cooked patty in her hand, Roberts says, "These cakes are good. If you eat these, you won't get hungry. I keep some in my pocket when I herd sheep. This is good old-time food."

NAVAJO TEA

It is obvious to us that Stella Worker enjoys quiet moments in the fields that surround her hogan. "I like to be outside with nature, walking the land." With her ever-present smile she says, "We come out here to the land for lots of things. Whatever I want or need I can have. It is all right here."

On this summer morning Stella has promised to make Navajo tea. Brewed from the Navajo plant known as "Cota" (*Thelesperma*), which grows abundantly on the reservation, the tea is said to be quite flavorful. Although the stems of the plant are usually ten- to thirty-centimeters long, with small leaves sprouting from the tops, only the leaves and stalks are used for the tea.

Stella searches along the road leading to her camp. She lingers in one spot for a short while in hopes of finding the plant. Without luck, she moves slowly on, explaining that "in the old days, when I was a little girl, we walked step by step with the sheep and looked for the tea. My eyes had to sort around the weeds to find it. Sometimes the tea tried to hide from me, but I always found it. These days my eyes aren't too good, so it is harder for me to find the plant."

She continues her slow pace, squinting, until she spots a cluster of plants in a grassy spot near a yucca. Smiling, Stella moves quickly toward the Navajo tea plant and uses her finger to carefully snap the plant stems. When she holds a bundle of seven plants in one hand, she declares, "It doesn't take much to make a good pot of tea."

Back at the camp, Stella fills a large pot with water and places it on her stove. Initially she is very talkative, but soon becomes absorbed by her work, lapsing into silence as she cleans each individual leaf and stem. When the water on the stove boils, Stella drops the plants into the pot, noting that "Navajo tea must cook awhile."

Ten minutes later the pink tea is deemed ready to drink. Steam rises from the pot and bright green stems float to the surface. Stella adds two teaspoons of sugar and stirs it into the tea. She lets it cool slightly and pours some into cups.

We drink the sweet tea until the pot is empty. Stella laughs at my appreciation of her tea made from plants. "I like this drink," she says. "Many women like it for their kids, to prevent them from drinking too much pop and coffee. I drink it year-round. Some people come and pick the tea and make a bundle of it. They dry it and put it in a gunnysack to use all winter. I do that, too." She pats her stomach. "This sure hits the spot. I love it. It's quick and easy and comes from our land."

Father Sky
embraces Mother
Earth, much as a
husband his wife.
Water flows
throughout the
world and
embraces the
earth,
propagating life.

Steven A. Darden

HAULING WATER

The community well that holds the water supply is in Blue Canyon, four miles from Roberta Black-goat's camp. The well sits in the center of rough tracks, which resemble a wheel with many spokes, each leading to a different homestead. Roberta must haul her water from this well or else from a spring eight miles from her camp, storing it in metal drums near her rockhouse and hogan. This is a difficult task and so she uses the water sparingly.

Roberta's water drums are filled once a week; today her son Danny will make a haul. First, he empties the remaining water from one drum to another. "I'm doing this pouring so the drum will be light, and it will be easier to put into the truck." As the water splashes into the drum, some of it accidentally spills onto the ground. Roberta sees water wasted and, with some exasperation, says, "Son, watch out for it! Use a big pan under the drum to catch the leftover. I'll use it for washing—every drop."

After Danny loads the empty drum into the back of his truck, we drive the bumpy road to the well. As he approaches a deserted camp where the logs of a hogan lie scattered on the ground, Danny explains that this is one of many old Blackgoat camps. His family has moved numerous times in search of better grazing areas for livestock. "This is something we Navajos do.

We follow the sheep. They need new grass, and so we have three or four camps spread out on our land. In spring, we take the sheep to our spring camp, the same for summer and fall. This way our sheep will have plenty to eat."

A few miles from the old camp, Danny points to another abandoned hogan. It is the place where he was born. Near the hogan spot is a large rock pile, the remains of what was once a make-believe fort for Danny. "We played cowboys and Indians there." He grows quiet again.

Clouds cast shadows on the bare rock walls of Blue Canyon. The community well is covered with sandstone and a pipe extends from its base ten feet into the air. Danny backs the pickup under the pipe, attaches the hose from the pipe to the barrel, and turns on the water. In ten minutes, the container is full. "There," he says. "Now we will have water for a while." This task complete, he drives slowly to Roberta's, promising he will take it easy on the bumps, careful not to spill a drop.

Back at camp, Danny uses a black rubber hose to siphon the water from the drum on the truck to one on the ground, which takes very little time. Roberta is pleased. "Now we have water to drink, cook, wash, and share with the dogs."

When the community well runs dry, Danny travels to a mountain spring eight miles from his mother's camp. "It's very comforting to know we'll always have a supply of water. We're lucky. When our well is dry, we can go to the spring. It always has water. We sometimes bring our sheep here to water. We're allowed to cross another's land in order to take our sheep and goats to drink. In the old days, we would race against our sheep to see who would get to the spring first. My brother and I would always win. Then the sheep would come baa-ing over the hill. They would drink to get cool, and we would pour water over our heads. The sun was very, very hot on the sheep and us. The water was very, very cold. The sheep didn't know they'd lost the race. Probably wouldn't care, either."

In the winter and spring, the Blackgoats do not have to haul water; instead, they use melted snow. During these months, a small stock tank is placed in the corral to catch rain and snow, which become drinking water for the animals. Buckets are left outside the hogan to collect water for cooking purposes. Danny explains, "We take water every way we can."

~~~

The corn grows up.
The waters of the dark clouds drop, drop.
The rain comes down.
The waters from the corn leaves drop, drop.
The rain comes down.
The water from the plants drop, drop.
The corn grows up.
The water of the dark mists drop, drop.

Song of Navajo Home God

The desert blooms whenever it rains. Therefore, to the Navajo, the seed in the ground waits for water to make it grow. The People value the water because it is a limited resource and they have developed certain patterns to help their crops grow. Ella Deal plants seeds in a valley not far from her summer camp. The winter and spring snows melt into the soil and keep it damp. Ella says, "The rain and snow bring us everything we need to get ready for the planting." With some luck, rain in the summer keeps the soil moist. From May until September, the Deals grow squash, melons, beans, and potatoes in their fenced garden that is an acre in size. "We have been using our land for about twenty years. This place has been good," Ella says.

One May morning, Helen and I arrive at the Deals' camp rather early. As Ella and her teenaged daughter Daisey lead us to plant beans, Ella glances up at the sky and says, "When you plant, it is best to come before the sun wakes up or you will roast."

She tromps through her fields, stopping to examine the small sprouts from earlier plantings that now are breaking through the ground. Ella passes the corn, potato, melon, and squash planting sections, stopping repeatedly to pull weeds surrounding the seedlings. As she works, she says, "This planting and keeping a garden is hard. There is always work to do. I have always helped with the planting. When I was with my mom and dad, my job was to scrape away the weeds. If you don't care for the vegetables and soil, then they will not be good. I used to help with the watering, too. My job was to water each plant and make sure it would not get thirsty. Our Navajo way is to spend time with our plants. We feed each one. We clean around each one, for these are the gifts of our mother earth. We must work together like partners to make it right."

Other Navajos use a variety of methods to grow healthy plants. Some farmers dig a six- to eight-inch cup around each plant so water will drain directly to the

seed. Others cover the seed with damp soil. Because the Southwest soil is so dry and water scarce, these techniques enable the seed to receive more water.

Ella walks to the northeast corner of the field. "This is my bean place. Today we'll put bean seeds in the ground." She picks up a long metal rod that leans against the fence. "This is a part of our old car. We use it now as our planting stick. The old people used a hard stick called greasewood. You push the stick deep into the earth to make a hole. Now you plant the seeds." Ella scrapes the weeds aside and pushes her modern planting stick into the soil, making a five-inch-deep hole. From a jar, she pours fifteen seeds into her hand and drops them in the hole. Surprised by the number, we ask her why she uses so many. She replies, "We have to make sure our plants grow. If the soil is dry, we put in lots of beans, like today, but if the dirt is really, really damp, then we put in just a few beans. When the dirt is soft, then it is really nice for planting." The women take turns, Daisey digging the next hole with the planting rod and Ella placing seeds in the soil. Daisey says, "We have to follow the rule with the planting. You must stay in a straight line. You face one way until you get to the end of the row, and you start the next row from that end. Then you have neat plants."

The women are hot after planting several rows of beans. Ella says, "It's time for a rest and fry bread and coffee. The sun always chases us indoors."

During the summer, when the soil becomes dry, the women carefully water each individual plant. "We mostly rely on the rains," Daisey says. "We're lucky because we live in the high country, and we get more rain than most Navajos, but when the dirt does get dry, then we haul water. We bring barrels of water down in a truck to the field. When it doesn't rain, we use a half-bucketful of water for each plant. We do this every day for a week at a time. We like wet, damp soil. Snow comes in the winter and gets the dirt real wet, but we have to help it along sometimes in the summer. When we do things right, then we have good crops."

One evening in July, we were invited to share dinner with the Deals. Ella and Daisey served huge platters of boiled corn on the cob and a bowl of steaming green beans. I devoured four ears and had three helpings of the fresh string beans. Ella joked that we would have to plant more the next day to replace all I had eaten.

In the fall the Deals have a tremendous task ahead of them as all the vegetables must be harvested before winter. The last beans are picked, and they begin to gather Indian corn, break squash from the vines, and dig new potatoes.

On a windy day in October, Ella and Daisey bring in the corn, checking each stalk and pulling off ears of corn. We notice this corn looks different from the summer corn—these are larger, with weathered leaves—so I break off an ear and push aside the husk. The various shades of red, yellow, white, and purple kernels surprise me. Daisey explains that this type of corn is used to make cornmeal patties. "We call this Indian corn, and we make many recipes with it."

Pale yellow, orange, pink, and green squash still lie on the ground, covered with leaves. Ella, Percy, and Daisey must tug and twist each squash until its stem breaks. Finally, Percy piles squash in the outstretched arms of his mother and sister, and they load up the pickup truck. Some of the squashes are so large that it takes two people to carry them.

The Deals harvest their potatoes last. Ella leads us to her favorite potato digging spot. She explains, "Fresh cracks in the ground mean the potatoes are ready. Now, watch me." Using her shovel, she digs into the soil, breaking the earth, and then triumphantly pulls up several pink potatoes with her hands. "I dig with a shovel and reach down and grab up the food. You can't dig too close to the plant or you will cut the potatoes under the ground. We always follow the planting line, then we know we'll get all the potatoes."

By late afternoon, small piles of fresh potatoes are scattered across the field. As we stop to rest, I notice that Ella has stopped digging and is sorting the potatoes into piles. "I put the potatoes into three piles. The largest potatoes we eat or give to friends; the middle-sized ones we give to the dogs; and the smallest we use for seeds next summer. The large potatoes and the small ones we store in our cellar. We store all our foods in there, then we can have vegetables to eat all year round."

It is still light when we return to her hogan, so we sit outside near the cottonwood trees. Ella is quiet for some time, staring at the ground, but gradually begins to talk, softly at first. "It is really nice to have a garden. When you don't have one, you get hungry for it. When you buy vegetables, you don't get much, and they don't taste the same." She pauses, her voice becoming stronger. "If we need help with the garden, then all our neighbors will come. We feed them. Everyone helps around here. These old people used to feed everyone and anybody and anyone. That is what my grandmother and grandfather told us to do. They told us to feed everybody who is hungry. You treat them that way, and they treat you that way. Nobody will ever go hungry here. My grandmother told me that they had hard days. Everybody in the area came

together and shared everything. Then everybody was okay. When we have a meeting, we bring food. Right now, meat is hard to get, but my family has plenty, so we bring meat to the squaw dances to share with The People. I am going to tell my children and everybody because we want this way to keep going and going.

"We even give people a place to sleep," Ella continues. "When you are around Navajos, they let you sleep where it is safe and warm. If you get stuck in the mud, someone will help. We take care of everyone. When you get to town, it is different. You have to pay to eat and sleep, even for a cup of coffee. In California, you even have to pay for a glass of water. Here, we share our home, our help, and our food."

〰

Wood is rooted in Mother Earth, the womb. She nourishes our wood and cares for it. Our wood and our trees project into Father Sky, and therein they, too, are nourished and strengthened. Wood provides shelter and warmth.

Steven A. Darden

FIREWOOD

It is a wintry morning, colder than usual for November, when we arrive at Roberta Blackgoat's camp. We greet each other with a hug instead of the previous handshake, and she invites us into her rockhouse for coffee and fry bread.

Often our inclination is to rush in and get started, but the Navajo custom is to sit in silence—sometimes for rather lengthy periods of time. Food is always offered, and it is considered an insult to refuse. Usually, we sit in silence until the host or hostess feels the moment is right to begin.

This time, Roberta tells her son Danny that it feels like snow and asks him to go to the wood-cutting spot to gather juniper. Roberta turns and smiles at us—she knows this is the task we have come to watch. Juniper and piñon are her main sources of heat. There are several advantages to these types of wood: they give off only small amounts of smoke, so the wood can be burned inside hogans, and they are quite hard and burn hot for long periods of time.

Danny drives his pickup to a juniper woodland about three miles from his mother's camp. An ominous feeling descends over me as the area appears to be a graveyard of dead trees and sage. The stark and lifeless juniper skeletons, sprawled throughout the area, remind me of hovering ghosts. All is silent and still, except for Danny, who surveys the trees, looking for a well-seasoned juniper.

He selects a large tree and swings his ax, stripping its small branches first and then cutting into the main trunk. Loud cracks echo, breaking the silence. Bits of juniper fly into the air, and Danny warns us to stand back. When he finishes, a large pile of branches and log chunks are all that remain. One chopped tree fills his entire pickup, but this supply will only last Roberta for a week.

When we return to Roberta's camp, we see her chopping wood, her skirt swinging back and forth as she cuts wide strokes in the juniper. Nearby, long juniper poles are piled in a curious fashion—like sheaves stacked tepee fashion. Roberta explains, "We put our wood this way so it will dry and become hard. In the winter, we will have the right kind of wood." She stands in silence for a few moments and then resumes her chopping. When she is finished, we carry in the cut wood and then help Danny unload the truck. As we work, Roberta says, "Tonight the outside will be cold, but the inside will be warm."

THE CORRAL

In a green valley not far from Dinnebito, Arizona, sits Oskar Whitehair's ranch, consisting of a large, pink stone house and two corrals. Seventy-two-year-old Oskar has a talent for building corrals. "I build my corrals strong and sturdy," he states.

Close to the house is a large corral made of juniper. "I can build these corrals in a day. First, I gather lots of cedar branches and logs, then I dig lots of postholes in the ground and make a great big circle. I push the cedar posts into the holes, then I take the branches and weave them together around the posts."

The pressure of the woven branches keeps the corral upright and tightly attached. Oskar uses neither nails nor wire to connect the branches. "It's kind of like putting a puzzle together. You have to fit the right pieces in the right places."

After the structure is finished, Oskar hangs old tin cans and dirty shirts on the corral fence. "I put these things up to keep the coyotes away. You see, the wind blows and the cans make noises that scare them. I hang up the shirts because the coyotes don't like man's smell. Our odor scares them away real fast."

Walking toward his second corral, Oskar says, "I'll build a new one when the ground in this old corral gets real dirty. I'll pick a spot that's flat and close to a tree. That way, the animals can get shade."

The sun is high and hot, but the animals inside this second corral, built around two piñon trees, appear cool. While most of the animals do not seem to notice us, one small lamb squeezes its head through the juniper branches of the corral and bleats loudly. "This one is just saying 'hi.'"

In the afternoon, we walk with Oskar to the open field to round up one of his flocks. "These sheep and goats live in the corral closest to my house." He whistles and yelps at the animals as they move along through the grasses. "These guys have been out getting fat, and it's time for them to come in and go to bed." The animals' hooves stomp the ground. Some walk slower than others, and Oskar becomes impatient and yells at them in Navajo to get along. As he opens the corral gate, the animals scurry in to drink from the water trough.

One by one, the sheep and goats begin to lie down to rest for the night. When they seem settled and quiet, Oskar bids them goodnight. As he walks back toward his house, he says, "My animals have a pretty good home."

SUMMER SHELTER

In late spring, Helen and I drive the desert roads near Dilcon, looking for Navajo summer shelters. Wildflowers and grasses outline the roads; in the distance are the Hopi buttes and the San Francisco Peaks.

The Navajo tradition is to build summer shelters that can withstand the winter months, leaving only minor repairs to be made for annual summer use. The original structure can easily be constructed in a half day. Juniper or piñon logs and boughs are used to build the shelter, which has four to six posts set in the ground in a rectangular shape. These main posts are connected by stringer posts, and the roof is made of long, thin poles that lie flat across the stringers. Covering the roof poles are the boughs. During the warm summer months, a Navajo family will move from its hogan to its summer shelter, an open-walled ramada that gives shade and allows free flow of the afternoon breezes.

Dilcon is a small reservation settlement with a trading post — both a general store and gas station — and a chapter house or community center and several prefabricated houses. We meet with a Navajo councilman, Manuel Shirley, an elected representative to Window Rock, the Navajo nation's capital. He tells us of a man named Yazzie who builds summer shelters and agrees to be our guide to Yazzie's camp.

We drive five miles over a double-lane dirt road to Yazzie's home, where we find a young man in his twenties on top of a summer shelter, fixing the roof. Manuel approaches the shelter as Yazzie jumps to the ground. While they talk, the councilman keeps pointing to the shelter and nodding, and soon Yazzie has agreed to talk about his work.

Yazzie is one of the few Navajos, of the many we have spoken with, whom we do not need to prod with questions. We are surprised by the willing openness of his explanations concerning the use and location of his summer shelters.

Every spring, Yazzie and his family move from their hogan to their summer shelter. "May is the time to start getting ready for the summer," says Yazzie. "Before I move my family into the shade, I always check it to make sure it is plenty strong. We live close to the south reservation border, and our summers are pretty hot these days. This shelter keeps us cool and not so sweaty."

Before the family moves to its summer home, Yazzie must rebuild parts of it. "Sometimes our winters are harsh and we lose roof poles and boughs. Our main posts stay still. They don't go anyplace. They've been in the ground now for about twelve years."

His old summer shelter is covered with brown, dried roof boughs, but the main posts, stripped of their bark, are thick. Yazzie inspects the sturdy structure and says: "We need only new boughs this year. Everything else is okay! When you make a summer home, you have to take your time and get good wood and cedar boughs. Good wood makes it last a long, long time. This summer shelter is old now and is still doing fine.

"When you build one, you have to go to the forest and cut down the fat cedar posts. For these, I go to Window Rock. I cut six fat posts that have a 'V' shape at the top. I call these the forked-end cedars. Then I cut about twenty skinny, tall posts and lots of cedar boughs. I load the wood and boughs in my pickup and drive them to the summer shelter place.

"To start, you have to dig holes about two feet deep and about six feet apart. You make a nice rectangle after the holes are in the ground, then I set in the fat cedar posts and have them stand tall and sturdy.

"Next, put lots of logs across the stringer poles to make a good roof and lay them about a half a foot apart. To make a good shade, cover the roof poles neatly with cedar branches and leaves. Make sure they lie flat to make the most shade for the shelter. To make even more shade, we lean some long poles against the roof. We put the poles on the west side and cover the poles with more cedar leaves and branches.

"Sometimes, in the old days, when it would get cold during the early fall, we put cedar branches around the bottom part of the shelter to keep us warm. This summer shelter here is half a modern one because we put plywood around it instead of cedar branches. I'll be taking down this plywood because we want to feel the breezes this summer and we don't want any vents. Then when September comes, I'll put the plywood back up."

Yazzie drives to a nearby forested area to gather fresh juniper boughs. With an ax, he cuts several large branches and loads them into his truck. Back at his summer home, he removes the dried, brittle boughs from the roof and tosses up the new ones, later arranging them neatly. He says: "Now we're ready for the summer. I'll move in a few beds, a shelf, a chest, some cooking utensils, and of course a lantern. I like living in this kind of home. When I was young, I would lay on my sheepskin at night and look up at the stars through the cedar leaves. It was good to see the moonlight shine through the roof and onto us. In the morning, I'd look up again and see the cedar posts and green leaves. Living in a shelter, it feels good to have the ground below and the cedar and its leaves surrounding me."

Animals are an ancient gift from the Holy People—*Diyin Diné*. When born, the animals are as infants. We, the Navajo, care for them through the process of herding. When they grow, they provide for us.

Steven A. Darden

MOCCASINS

Sam Worker is a well-known moccasin maker in the Leupp, Arizona, area. His uncle taught him the craft when he was a small boy, and now, at the age of sixty, Sam spends his days cutting and sewing cowhide to supply moccasins for his family and the community.

Helen and I visit Sam and his wife, Stella, whose camp lies about five miles from a paved highway. Our arrangements are to meet Sam at the intersection of his dirt-road turnoff and the highway so he can guide us to his camp since it would be difficult for us to find it on our own. As we drive up, we see a Navajo man in a gray pickup truck parked at the turnoff. Helen and I assume it is Sam. We wave and turn onto the dirt road. He makes no acknowledging motion, not even a nod. He simply turns around and heads toward his camp, driving sixty miles an hour. It seems as if he is running away from us. We cannot see Sam but try to follow his dust trail, with no luck. We come to several forks in the road and attempt to find fresh tire tracks, but our guesses are always wrong. Helen and I must have traveled more than fifteen miles, passing over two wooden bridges. Since the Worker camp is only five miles from the highway, obviously, we are lost. We drive into the next camp where, fortunately, the inhabitants speak English. They know the Workers and are able to give us

directions. We are relieved to finally see the hogan "with the trees in front," as we know it is where Sam and Stella live.

Our first meeting is awkward. As we share details of our circuitous journey with them, Stella laughs and tells us, "We Navajos know all the parts of our land and where our people live. We know the rocks, the trees, the plants, and the hills. The map is in our heads." In this way, she excuses Sam's behavior.

The day we spend with Sam and Stella is quiet as they sit working in their hogan: Stella at her loom, brushing down yarn and weaving; Sam on his mat, surrounded by tools, cowhide, and buckskin. He is now ready to sew a gift for his wife—a pair of moccasins.

Silently, Sam spreads a piece of six-by-twelve-inch cowhide on the floor and, using a sharp knife, cuts the outline of the sole. While he works, Stella explains how Sam readies the hide: "Go out to the field and find a cow. Let its hide lie in the sun. It needs to dry. Sam cuts the good part of the hide to make it soft, then buries the hide strip in the sand. The sand is wet. This makes it soft. It stays in the sand for about two days. When he takes it out of the sand, he scrapes off the cow fur. Now it is ready to make a shoe."

Sam's hands shake as he pulls the hide tightly in order to stretch it. He molds the hide onto a concave

board. There, he hammers it to round the sole into the shape of a foot. When the hide needs to be softened, he dips it in a bowl of water. Next, Sam uses buckskin, purchased from the trading post, for the upper part of the moccasin. As he puts the long section of pre-cut skin on top of Stella's foot and around her ankle, it forms the shape of a shoe. Satisfied that the buckskin piece is the correct size, Sam joins the two skins to form the moccasin.

He begins to sew. Using the awl, he punches two holes in the cowhide and one hole in the buckskin. With his fingers, instead of a needle, he laces the buckskin upper to the cowhide sole. While he punches and stitches, his hands work in a rhythm, using the pulled-down-stitch method. He tugs and pulls each stitch separately to tighten it. Making a pair of moccasins takes about three hours; Sam works quickly and precisely.

As he sews, Stella tells us about their lives. "We love our land," she says. "There's no place just like this here. All my kids were born here except for one. My husband was born on this land and so was his mother. I was a sheepherder. Sam was a sheepherder, too, and he worked for the railroad but then hurt his back very, very bad. Because he hurt himself, he cannot work for the railroad or be a sheepherder. Now he makes moc-

casins all day long. His uncle told him how to make moccasins. He's been making them since he was a boy."

In Sam's youth, he used a natural thread made of sinew, which is a tendon from a deer, goat, or sheep. He would stretch and moisten the tendons and twist the fibers together to form a thin thread. Over the years, Sam has changed material and now uses fishing line to sew the skins together.

When Sam finishes sewing the buckskin to the cowhide, he pushes a long stick inside the shoes and presses it against the seams. With a hammer, he taps the seams against the stick, rounding and blending each buckskin seam. His hands rub, shape, and mold the moccasin so it will fit Stella's foot; he then removes the moccasin, rinses it in water, and wraps it in a wet towel. Stella says, "It's easy to sew and shape the hide when it's wet. When it's dry, you can't do anything."

Sam continues working on the second moccasin. He uses the same procedure—punching holes, threading hide, and tugging the fish line. He does not rest or stretch until he has finished.

Stella sits close by, working at her loom. "We spend our days like this. I weave and Sam sews. There are just two of us now. Our children are all grown up. Sometimes they come to visit and sometimes our grandchildren come to visit. We have a big family. Some of my children live on the reservation and some off. We are happy when they come back to our land." The land is obviously synonymous with home.

When Sam finishes sewing both shoes, Stella slips on the moccasins. Sam measures the place for three buttonholes and cuts the leather. Next, he fastens the buttons. At last, her moccasins are ready to be worn.

"When the moccasins are new, you have to wear them right away to have them take shape," Stella says. "You keep them on until it gets dark, way into the evening. You can put oil on them to keep them soft. When you wear them all of the time, you get used to it and you know your feet will be warm. When I was a little girl, I didn't wear shoes, just moccasins. Later, when I got a pair of white man's shoes, my friends called my feet big dippers. They would say, 'Hey, where did you get those big dippers?' Now I only wear moccasins. They feel good."

BRANDING

In the distance from Ella and Leonard Deal's camp, gathered around a water hole, one hundred head of cattle graze their land. One summer afternoon, Ella drives us out to the water hole where steers, heifers, and calves drink and rest.

The Deals' cattle require little care. Leonard tends the herd weekly "by counting the cows and looking them over to make sure they are okay." Ella says, "These cows are easy to have. They're good and they know how to behave. They don't run off very much." Most of the year the animals eat reservation grasses, but when snows are heavy Leonard has to feed them hay. During the winter and spring, the calves are born; in the summer, the Deals have to brand them.

Branding, a cooperative effort for the entire Deal family, involves more planning and organization than any other task. The grown children return to help. Ella says, "Branding our cows is hard. There are many jobs to do. Everyone helps. If you come to watch, we make you work. No one sits."

The event takes place in a special corral that is used only for branding. Ella's family built the corral when she was a small child. One hundred feet in diameter, the corral's hard juniper branches have been tightly woven together. Through the years, various parts of the structure have been rebuilt, but, sixty years later, this corral is still used by Ella and her family.

On branding day, all family members are awake by sunrise. After breakfast, Ella's grandchildren take the horses to the corral to await the action. At the camp, Ella and her daughters, Daisey and La Vern, and her daughter-in-law, Christine, make hominy stew, which will simmer all day over a fire in order to be ready after the branding. The women fill a large ice chest with soft drinks and ice water and load it into Ella's pickup. Leonard, his son-in-law, Tom, and Percy load ropes, branding irons, and juniper wood into Leonard's truck. The family climbs into the two pickups and drives to the corral.

They move quickly to get ready for the branding. The women unload the trucks as the men build a fire. Soon the flames roar and the heat is strong—a hot fire is needed to heat the branding irons. As the fire burns to red coals, Percy and Leonard ride to a nearby mesa to round up the herd and push the slow-moving cattle toward the corral. Once inside, the cows begin to move in a circle. Thick dust rises as the animals continue their pacing. Although only the calves are to be branded, the men bring all the cattle into the corral. Christine says, "The branding is just for the babies, but we have to bring everyone in so the babies will come in, too."

When the cattle are inside the corral, Christine places several different brands in the red coals. The heifer brand is **OO**, the steer brand is **ST**, and a third brand worn by both steers and heifers is **─N**, the Navajo tribal symbol. Next, she quickly covers dirt across a section of each rod to keep the heat from traveling up the handle. After a few minutes, the branding irons change from black to red.

While the branding irons heat, the men select a large male calf from the moving herd. Tom twirls a lasso in the air and throws it over the calf's neck, then quickly braces the rope around his own body and moves toward the branding post. This post, usually located in the center of the corral, is used to secure the rope and calf. With the help of other men, he pulls the rope and wraps it around the post as the calf struggles to get free. Tom then lassos the calf's hind legs. As the men push the bawling calf down on its side, Percy calls for the branding iron. Christine passes it over the fence to Ella, who hands the hot iron to Percy. Leonard and Tom hold the rope while Percy sears the animal's rump. Smoke rises from its singed fur and hide as the calf bawls and his eyes bulge. Percy tags the young male's ear and then ties a length of rubber tubing around the testicles to neuter the calf.

The branded calf looks rather stunned. As the men loosen the ropes, the animal jumps up and stumbles back to the herd in search of his mother. Christine comments, ''Some cows cry and yell and some are quiet. Some act like they don't even care.''

Next, Leonard selects a second male calf. The men rope, wrestle, brand, tag, and neuter the husky animals. ''We brand the big babies first,'' Ella says. ''Some cows have babies in the winter and some in the spring. We brand the largest ones first because they are strong and they have more energy. When we start, we have more energy, too! Then we finish with the smaller ones.''

At one point during the branding, Ella makes a count and notices a few cows missing. She asks Daisey and La Vern to round up the remaining animals, so the young women leave their job, recording the number of heifers and steers branded, and ride east on horseback toward the cornfields. An hour later, they return with ten nervous cows. When the animals reach the corral gate, they refuse to enter. The men push all the cattle back outside of the corral to mingle with the strays. A minute later, the men herd all the cows back inside. Christine explains, ''Some of the cows don't want to go into the corral. Even though they are not getting branded, they remember when they did. But cows like company, so if all the cows are coming into

the corral, even the stubborn ones will feel safe enough to follow."

During the day, the family repeats the branding process forty-five times. The air is hot and dusty, and the cows continually pace inside the corral. Except for a few breaks, the Deals work constantly.

By mid-afternoon, the branding is finished. After checking to see that all the calves have brands, Ella opens the gate and the men push the cattle back into the fields. While Christine puts out the fire, everyone else helps load the gear into the trucks. The grandchildren ride the horses back to the camp as the trucks follow.

Back at the camp to rest and eat, Ella is glad to find her hominy stew still simmering on the wood-burning stove inside her hogan. "After a hard day, it is good that we don't have to come back here and cook. The food is already ready." The family relaxes under the shade tree near the hogan, eating stew and yeast rolls and chatting about the day's events. The cows and their newly branded calves graze in the nearby fields. The branding is over for another year.

HERDING

I put this livestock here for you; it is your father and your mother, your thoughts and your mind. You will have children and grandchildren and so forth as time goes on. Your livestock is going to be your life.

Relocation Booklet, Teesto, Arizona

Ella and Leonard Deal are also sheepherders. Thirty years ago, Ella's father gave them a flock of ten sheep and two goats as a wedding gift. Today, their herd numbers one hundred and fifty sheep and goats, an important source of income for the family. The surplus animals are either sold at auctions or butchered and their wool sold or used for weaving.

Ella, her daughter Daisey, and I stand outside the Deals' hogan this morning and watch Leonard in the distance as he herds their flock of animals back to camp. The white coats of the sheep and goats contrast sharply with the green fields. Ella says, "The sheep and goats got up early this morning, and they have been grazing, just eating grass and drinking water." Leonard moves the animals back toward the corral as Ella continues, "He knows when it's time to bring them back because they are missing home, and it's getting too hot for them." During the warm weather, sheep and goats graze in the early morning and evening when it is cool, but in the spring, fall, and winter, the animals graze from mid-morning to noon and from afternoon to sunset.

As Leonard swings a lasso and yells to the animals to move on, a sheepdog leads the parade through sage and rabbit brush. Three other dogs harass the herd, snapping at their heels. While the dogs bark loudly, the animals bleat in complaint and stomp their feet in rebellion. Heads bobbing in objection, the animals kick up clouds of dust as they enter the corral.

Once inside, the babies nestle close to their mothers to nurse. Leonard checks the flock, crooning to them. After feeding their lambs and kids, the sheep and goats cluster together in the shade of the corral walls. All is quiet. Leonard closes the gate and says goodbye softly, returning to his hogan for a cup of coffee and rest. It is time to return to the peaceful part of the sheepherder's life.

All of the elder Deals herd sheep, and many hours are spent with the animals. "Sometimes it can be a boring job," Daisey says. "When my mom is with the sheep, she brings her wool and spins and cards it. I bring a book, and my dad does leather work. We can fill the time and get two jobs done at once. Even though we're busy, we still keep an eye on the sheep."

The Deal family life revolves around their sheep in order to prevent overgrazing damage to the land. The family moves with the flock to a different camp every season. "We move from camp to camp and move the sheep, too. They go where we go because then we can find them lots of food," Daisey says. "We used to move all four seasons, but now we don't have to. We only have three hogans because the hogan at our fall camp is too old and broken down. We're not worried, though. We know our sheep get enough grass from three moves." Each camp is a home, complete with hogan, shed, and corral. The winter camp is located in a forested area of their land, but the spring and summer camps are on flatter terrain. "In the winter, we take our sheep to the mountain. They eat trees and leaves up high because the ground is covered with snow. In the summer, they eat in the flat areas."

The sheep eat rabbit brush, greasewood, piñon, and juniper. Ella says, "My sheep eat many kinds of grasses. We chase them to the salty weeds up on the mountain. If you don't chase them up there, they will eat dirt! We're lucky to have enough for the sheep to eat, but we do worry about finding enough water for them. When we herd, we listen to the animals and do what they want to do. Sometimes they want to drink and drink, and in the winter they eat snow for water. We can't always count on water in the summer. The hole dried out last summer, and we had no water. The tribe had to haul water to us."

Aside from worrying about the scarcity of water, the Deals must protect their sheep from wild animals. "It's best to stay with your sheep. If we just let them run around, then the coyotes get them. So far, we've lost two lambs this summer. The coyotes don't kill just one sheep. They kill one and then keep on trying to kill them all. You have to watch for foxes, too. Most of the time, the sheep don't run off. We chase them across the wash and then they eat their way home."

In addition to watching the herd on a daily basis, the Deals have seasonal tasks to perform, such as tending the ewes at lambing and shearing in the spring. "We [three women] shear before it gets hot. It took us twenty-five days to shear our sheep. We're busy," Ella says. Also in the summer, the family dips their sheep with a chemical solution that controls pests and skin diseases. "The tribe has a place near our area where we can go and dip our sheep. We usually dip after the Fourth of July. Some of our sheep might carry a bug,

so we give them a shot and put them through the dip."

Family members, including the children and the elders, help with the herding, lambing, shearing, and dipping. Learning to care for livestock is considered an important maturing process for young Navajos. The Deals' sheep and goats are both a source of livelihood and a source of pride. With a smile, Ella says, "When you're able to care for yourself and your sheep, you are grown. It's hard to keep sheep, but we like them. We're proud that we have them. My children get hungry for mutton. They come home and butcher. They get homesick for it, and we're glad we have our sheep and goats."

COOKING A GOAT

Sheep and goats are vital to the Navajos as sixty percent of their diet consists of products from these animals. Sixty-two-year-old Roberta Blackgoat recognizes the vital importance of her goats and sheep: "They are my food. We eat every part of the goat or sheep. We use everything. When we don't eat the meat, we miss it. We don't have to go to the store and buy it. It is all right here for us."

Today Roberta says she is hungry for ribs, liver, and blood cakes, which she makes from her sheep or goats. Helen and I arrive early and we all walk to the corral, where her flock is kept for the night. Roberta examines the animals with a knowing eye until she finds a fat goat to butcher. Tying a rope around its neck, she drags it close to her hogan. The animal begins to object as it is forced to the ground. Roberta steadies its shoulder with her foot as the goat bleats in protest. With a knife, she slits its throat—one quick slash. Observing this custom brings us closer to understanding Roberta's attitude toward animals. She explains: "This is my way of living, and it is a part of being close to the earth."

After the slaughter, Roberta pulls the carcass onto a plastic garbage bag and puts a large bowl under the goat's slit neck to collect the blood. With a knife, she cuts open the chest and lower body, removing the intestines, stomach, pancreas, liver, and heart. She also cuts out the ribs, transferring these body parts onto a second plastic sheet, for these are ingredients she will use today.

Roberta drags the plastic, loaded with goat parts, into her hogan. Helen and I follow, carefully carrying the bright red blood in a white bowl. Roberta says, "It's time to start cooking." She builds a small juniper fire, adding sticks to the flames "so the fire will make a good bed of coals." Her stove is an oil drum cut in half with a metal pipe attached to the flat top that runs up to an opening in the ceiling. While the fire burns down, she cuts the goat ribs into four sections. Once this task is complete, Roberta drops the ribs onto a grill that sits in front of her stove. They sizzle as they hit the grill, and soon the air is heavy with the smell of juniper and cooking meat.

As the ribs cook, Roberta holds up both the small and large intestines and says, "I'll make goat links with these." She asks us to check the ribs while she takes the intestines outside, where she pushes the partially digested grass out of each strip and then rinses the string in cold water. When she returns, she takes the two intestine strips and wraps them around her finger as a starter link. When the link is formed, she removes her finger, twists the long intestines, and continues the

curling and wrapping motion. "You have to do a good job and make it neat." The intestine is wrapped in a foot-long coil and then placed on the grill next to the ribs. She repeats the process until all the intestines have been used.

Roberta pays attention to detail in her cooking. The ribs are all cut exactly the same width, and the goat links are wrapped tightly, one link on top of the other. The ribs and links are evenly arranged in a straight line across the grill.

As the ribs and the links roast, Roberta turns to her next task. "When I cook a goat, I have to be quick and do two or three jobs at a time. You have to make sure you get to cook as much as you can so as not to waste anything." She pauses. "So I'll start to make the blood cakes. This is good food."

Roberta separates the lining of one of the goat's four stomachs from its muscle layers. She carefully lifts the bowl full of goat blood and pours it into the lining. The sack bulges but not a drop spills. Roberta calmly places the full sack back in the bowl, making sure the opening is closed and folded over.

When the ribs and links are grilled, we take a break from cooking and have a late brunch, eating meat right off the grill. Both the ribs and the links have a similar taste, greasy and sweet with the flavor of burning juniper. Too soon the grill is empty.

It is now time to move on to Roberta's rockhouse. We carry the goat carcass and the bowl with the sack of blood to her kitchen, which is slightly larger, has more cooking utensils, and a stove with an oven. Roberta says she feels more comfortable here. She spends most of her time in this two-room rock structure, where one room has four beds and the other is a large family kitchen.

Once Roberta is settled, she prepares the next recipe, a liver dish. She begins by pinching and squeezing a second goat stomach until it becomes soft and juicy. When the stomach is just right, she walks outside to empty the juice. As it pours out, some spills onto her hands. Roberta's eyes grow large and she hurries back inside, grabbing a wet towel to wipe off the hydrochloric acid, a harsh digestive juice. "The wet inside the stomach sure hurts my hands, so I get it off really, really fast."

When the stomach is clean, Roberta makes stuffing for the inside. First, she tears the goat liver, fat, and leftover intestines into small bits. As she works, she tells stories concerning different parts of the goat. She holds up the rumen, similar to the gizzard, and says, "Men don't eat this. If they do, they are the first to get lost in a war or the first to get shot." As she shows the

sternum and goat nipples, she explains, "If teenagers eat these, then they will have bumps on their faces—I mean, pimples." Roberta takes the bile ducts off the liver. "If you eat this, you will go blind."

She picks up the shredded liver and fat and squeezes them together. "I add a little bit of salt," she says as she measures it into her palm. Then using her hands, she stuffs the mixture into the soft stomach. Roberta works quickly and every movement is exact. Soon the bag bulges, and she ties a cheesecloth strip around the stomach opening. The stuffed stomach sausage resembles a large gray cheese. "Now you can cook it lots of different ways. You can roast it on a grill in your hogan, you can boil it in water, or you can dig a pit outside, build a fire in the pit, and let it bake." Today, she chooses to boil it on her wood-burning stove.

Roberta puts a few inches of water with the stuffed stomach in a large pot and stokes the stove with juniper wood. The fire heats quickly and warms the room. After the water boils, she turns the stuffed stomach several times so it will cook thoroughly. The room smells of freshly cooked meat. She hardly pauses for breath before starting the next recipe.

Roberta repeats, "We use all but a little of the goat or sheep," emphasizing just how essential these animals are to the Navajos. She adds, "We even take the fat after it melts and put it in the can [an old Crisco can]. I use it as shortening for fry bread. We take the goat head, boil it, and eat the meat. It tastes good, and we are healthy."

While the liver sausage boils, Roberta takes the heart and pancreas outside and puts these parts on a rack to dry in the sun and fresh air. "These foods hang on a wood rack, which is up very high so animals, such as coyotes, dogs, and bobcats, cannot get them."

Roberta turns the organs every few hours so the sun will dry them thoroughly. If the air is dry, the process takes one full day but may take as long as two or three days if the air is damp. She brings the organs indoors during the night.

It is now time to make Navajo blood cakes. We have been anticipating this event all day. Most of the afternoon, our eyes were on Roberta, but every now and then they would wander over to the goat stomach full of blood. She turns to me and says, "Now, I have been saving the best for last." Roberta unties the stomach lining and pours the blood into a bowl. Next, she peels three potatoes, slices them crisply into thin pieces, and dumps them into the bowl. She tears off sections of goat fat, drops them into the mixture, and adds three large handfuls of cornmeal. Roberta stirs the mixture with her hands and watches as the cornmeal thickens the liquid, then explains, "I add a small handful of pepper, a sprinkle of onion salt, a handful of salt, a little bit of chile powder, and a few chopped chile peppers." Her hands slowly stir the mixture.

The fire in Roberta's cook stove burns low, so she adds more wood and warms a heavy cast-iron skillet. Next, she rubs the skillet with goat fat, pours in the mixture, and puts the skillet in her oven to bake. Soon the delicious aroma of potatoes, meat juices, and seasonings fills the air. Thirty-five minutes later, Roberta removes the baked blood cake from the oven. The watery red batter emerges as a solid, dark brown cake. As melted goat fat sputters around the sides, she places the hot skillet to cool on a pile of dry firewood stacked near the stove. Moments later, she slices the cake into long, thick wedges for us all to taste. It is bland, wholesome, and heavy—quite a surprise!

Roberta traditionally makes fry bread to accompany the goat feast. She makes the dough with her hands. "Oh, I don't cook exact. I cook by feeling and I put lots in my fry bread. I put four handfuls of bread flour in a bowl with a little bit of baking powder, a little bit of salt, and some warm water—just a little at a time—then I mix it together with my hands. I might use a little more water and a little more flour to get it right."

While the lard boils, she makes balls of dough and shapes them into large flat pancakes. She then slaps the dough back and forth, stretching it around her hand into a paper-thin pancake, which she drops flat into the hot grease. The dough quickly bubbles and starts to rise. Three minutes pass before Roberta turns it over. After the bread cooks to a golden brown, she removes it from the skillet. She fries the remaining dough in the same manner, and when she is finished, six crisp rounds of fry bread cool in a bowl. "I like to top the bread with salt or honey."

Roberta has just spent the entire day cooking a goat. She shares some of it with her son, Danny, and her neighbors. This was a day of hard work, and now it is time to relax and enjoy the feast.

HORSE HOBBLE

One late October day, Sally Gordy takes us to her parents' camp, near Black Mesa, Arizona, where her father is well-known for his leather work, in particular, horse hobbles. We had seen the Gordys' horses grazing as we approached their camp. The horses are kept in a corral during the night but are free to roam during the day. Joe Gordy is proud of his five horses. "They are good animals. I don't have to watch them all the time. I can kind of trust them, except for one. He is on the wild side, and so he gets a horse hobble to keep him under control."

A horse hobble is a strip of leather that fits securely around the horse's forelegs. Once the horse is put in the hobble, it is able to step with its back legs but can only hop with its front pair. Joe says, "I can tie the strip around the horse's legs to keep him gentle, then he can't run far."

Joe stretches a one-by-eighteen-inch cowhide strip tightly across a nearby log. "This hide has been buried in the damp ground to make it soft. It is easier to work with now." Holding a sharp knife with his fingertips, he scrapes the hair off the hide. As Joe removes the hair, he says, "Way back in the old days, we used to scrape the hide with a stone to get rid of the hair. I learned this [way] from my father's uncle." After the final scrapes, the hide is clean and its texture rough.

Tanning, the Navajo way, is a lengthy process. Joe explains, "It takes lots of work. After I scrape off the fur, then I tan the hide. I cure it and work it over. I hit it against the trees. You always keep it moving." Joe demonstrates this technique and stretches the hide under his foot. He repeats, "I always keep it moving to make it get soft. If I don't, it becomes hard. At night, I do let it sleep. It is wrapped in a wet rag to keep the air and the dry out." He continues to work the hide and then hands it to his wife, Alberta. "I need a rest," he laughs. Alberta folds and twists the strip, then slaps it against a woodpile. The hide is never motionless in her hands.

While Alberta works the strip, Joe takes out some cooking oil and pours it into his palms. When Alberta hands him the hide, he lavishly applies it to the leather. "I rub cooking oil into the hide. Old people used animal brains, or you can use bone marrow. This oil makes the strip easier to twist and shape."

Joe buries the cowhide again in the soil. The moisture must slowly penetrate the skin in order to make it pliable. "You want to get the wetness into it, but you don't want it to go very fast. You want the soil damp but not too full of water. This cowhide will stay in the ground for one to two days." Joe cautions, "If the hide doesn't feel right when you take it out, then you have to bury it again and tan it until it gets right." Taking a shovel, Joe scoops out a few mounds of damp soil, places the leather in the ground, and covers it thoroughly.

Alberta invites us in to the summer shelter for coffee and fry bread. As Joe sips coffee, he continues with the horse hobble lesson: "We will leave that strip buried in the wet soil for a few days, then dig it up, pull it out, and shake it clean. It is now ready to become a hobble. However, today I'll show you with this rawhide."

Joe takes a strip of leather from a bag. "First, I tie a knot at one end of the strip, then I cut a half-inch slit at the other end. Close to the center of the strip, I will fold over part of it to make a loop. Now this loop is the size of a horse's leg. You want the loop slightly bigger than the horse's leg, so you must allow it to give a little.

"Then I hold the loop together with my fingers and let the rest of it hang below my hand. I put the loop over a log and twist the hanging strips together real tight, making a five-inch middle strap. You have enough strip left over after the twisting to make a second loop. This second loop has the knot and slit, so I hook the two together. That's it. Our horse will use a hobble like this for a long time. When I make the buried leather into a hobble, it will dry in the sun and be ready for my wild horse. I'll have to be tough with my horse when I put my horse hobble on him. At least, he won't go far now.

"I like to make horse hobbles. They are really from the old days and the old ways. My uncle taught me to take my time, work slowly, and do it right. He told me that to really work the leather, you need to keep it moving. My uncle taught me a lot about leather. I'm glad he did."

A fine quality Navajo rug includes both a tight weave and an intricate design. Hazel Nez, a weaver from the Big Mountain area, is well-known for her beautifully crafted rugs. Hazel lives alone in a big, mesa-top camp which consists of a hogan, a corral, a weaving shed, and two houses. Above the door of one of the houses is a wooden sign: Hazel K. Nez.

Hazel is extremely knowledgeable, having been a weaver for more than forty years. She explains that her mother taught her how to weave: "She stood over me and watched until I did it right." She continues, "It takes me about two months to make a rug, but of course it depends on the size. I take all the things from around me to make a rug. I love to weave. I love to spend my time with the weaving."

There are many time-consuming steps to prepare the wool before the actual weaving may begin. Helen and I ride with Hazel to her sheep camp in order to watch the sheepshearing. As we travel over the bumpy dirt road, Hazel explains, "We always shear in the spring. You can't shear too early or the sheep will get cold."

After greeting her family members, Hazel and her six-year-old grandson, Sonny, emerge from the hogan with ropes in hand. Hazel motions us to follow them toward the sheep grazing in a nearby field. As Sonny runs around the flock, he whistles, yelps, and skips, and the animals slowly begin to move toward the camp.

Hazel's eyes scan the flock looking for an old male to shear first. She throws a lasso around the sheep's head and says, "I've done pretty good on my first try." After pulling the frightened animal away from the herd, she ties his legs together and gently pushes him over on his side. Hazel's grandson holds the sheep's head in one hand, strokes the animal's nose with his fingers, and speaks quietly in Navajo to calm him. Hazel tells us, "When I was a young child, my job was just like my grandson's. I had to hold the sheep's head to keep him quiet so that my mother could shear."

Hazel takes her long metal shears and begins cutting wool in the sheep's chest area. Over and over, the shears clip, cutting sections of the animal's fleece free. After the wool is removed from the chest, she snips the wool from the shoulders and hind legs. Shearing the fleece with one hand, she holds the solid wool piece in the other. With one side finished, Hazel and her grandson flip the sheep over.

When the second side is shorn, Hazel gives the sheep a pat on the back and unties his legs. The sheep jumps up, shakes, and trots off to the herd, baa-ing

loudly. Hazel laughs and says, "Oh, he is calling to his friends and telling them that he is clean and nice and cool." She wraps the wool into a bundle and stuffs it into a bag. "Now, let's go back to my house and clean it."

Inside, Hazel begins the washing of the wool. She shakes the fleece vigorously, spreads it on the floor, and picks out small burrs and sticks. At last, she speaks. "These sheep can pick up lots of stuff while they are grazing. This coat is very dirty, so it needs to be cleaned with soap and water." After dumping a bucket of water into a washtub, she throws the fleece into the tub and lets the wool soak. She empties the dirty water and repeats this cold-rinse process four times. Next, Hazel washes the fleece, adding warm water from the kettle on the stove. This time, she uses detergent, rinses the fleece, and hangs it out on a nearby fence. After a few hours, the warm Arizona sun has dried the fleece and it is ready for carding.

Carding is the process of straightening the wool fibers before they are spun. Hazel uses two wooden tow cards, flat paddles of plywood made with wooden handles and metal teeth, to comb the fleece. She sits on a goatskin close to her house and takes up her tow cards and a small piece of wool. She places the wool in the metal teeth of one card, and with the other card begins to comb the fibers. Back and forth, Hazel transfers the wool from one card to another, brushing the fibers until they are straight. As she cards, she says, "It takes me about two weeks to card enough wool for a rug. If you card slow, then you never get tired. You must always have to think that you are going to card or spin or weave more. There is always a job to do." She continues carding until the wool comes off of the cards in fluffy strips called batts. "Pretty soon, I'll have a nice big pile of soft wool ready to spin."

Throughout the next two weeks, Hazel cards all of her wool into a soft, fluffy pile. Finally she declares, "This wool is ready for spinning." Spinning transforms the carded batts into yarn; the spindle is the tool used for this task. Hazel brings out her drop-spindle and a bag full of wool batts. As she sits on the front step in the sun, where her dogs and cats rest close by, she twirls the spindle once and attaches a yard of yarn to show me how easily and smoothly it goes around. She then picks up a wool batt and attaches it to the tip of the spindle, spinning the stick with one hand and tugging the fibers from the batt with the other. The batt changes quickly into a thick, airy piece of yarn. She twists this fat yarn around the spindle, making the yarn tighter. Hazel continues to pull the yarn off the spindle with a downward motion, until it attains a fine texture. All is quiet except for the humming of the spindle. Hazel's hands appear to be dancing. She extends her feet in front of her, with heels to the ground and toes in the air, wrapping the spun yarn around them. She continues the spinning for several hours and then stops for the day. When she stands up, Hazel says, "I'll spin again tomorrow and maybe the next day. The spinning for one rug will take a couple of weeks. Like I said before, when you weave, you always have a job to do."

After the wool is spun, it must be washed a second time. "You just can't get it too clean," Hazel says. She pours water into a large kettle and heats it on the stove. When the water is hot, she puts it in a metal bowl and adds some cold water to make it lukewarm. "If you wash wool in really hot water, it shrinks. The wool won't be any good. If it shrinks, it gets coarse." She adds detergent to the water and soaks the yarn. It blends with the soapsuds as Hazel swishes, rubs, and squeezes it. "We used to use yucca to wash the wool. Today, I use Tide. In the old, old days, my grandma used yarn as big as fingers because she never washed it to make it clean. It would be fat from the dirt."

Hazel rinses the wool thoroughly after several washings. The last rinse water is clean. "My water is clear because the wool is clean," she says proudly. When she wrings the yarn with both hands, clean water falls to the floor. "Now I'll hang it up to dry." Hazel takes the skeins of yarn outside and walks toward her juniper post fence. "This is my drying fence. I'm going to wrap the wet wool around the fence posts so the wool will dry." She attaches the yarn to one fence post and walks back and forth, wrapping the yarn from that fence post to the next. A slight breeze moves the yarn as it dries on the fence.

After wrapping the wool, Hazel says, "Next, I check for lumps and take them off the wool." Her fingertips run along the wool, removing the small bumps. "I wrap the yarn so it stretches and becomes all the same size. If you don't stretch the yarn, then it comes out fat and thin. It can really change sizes on you, and that doesn't make for weaving a good rug."

Hazel begins the long task of unwinding the dry, clean yarn after removing the knots from the wool. Back and forth, she walks, looping the yarn around her hand and arm. As she removes the skein from her elbow and loops it over to form a neat bundle, she says, "Like I told you before and I'll tell you again, there is lots to do when you weave."

Hazel's wool has been sheared, washed, carded, spun, and washed a second time. The next step is to dye it. She uses several different methods to obtain her variety of colors. She may create natural wool tones from blending the light and dark aniline dyes, or she often uses plant dyes made from bark, roots, and fruit. Occasionally, Hazel might use a store-bought dye, but she explains, "I like to dye using the things from the land. Sometimes we spend a day gathering plants to use for the dyes. I take my grandkids and we have a picnic. You can make lots of different colors from the plants and things." Hazel takes great delight in this aspect of the weaving process.

She plans to use shades of white, gray, black, red, and brown in her next rug. "The white and black are easy. They just come from the black and white sheep. For brown, I use wild walnuts. The red dye I buy from the store." She has traveled to Oak Creek Canyon, Arizona, more than two hundred miles from her home, to collect the walnuts. "I let those nuts soak overnight and then I boil them in the morning, maybe for two hours. The water turns dark, dark brown. I add the wet yarn and boil it some more. I take it off the heat and let it soak and cool. It soaks for a few days, then I take it out of the pot and rinse it until I know the dye is stuck into the yarn. I let it dry and then wind it up in a ball. It is ready for the weaving."

Hazel enters the weaving shed and stands by her loom. "This is it! This is where I do my work, my weaving work." The large piñon [pine] posts of the loom are notched together to form a rectangle; the heavy lower posts act as a base.

As she prepares the loom, Hazel explains, "The first thing I do is string the warp threads onto the warp frame." The warp threads are the foundation of the rug, and the warp frame is a separate piece of the loom, complete with two posts and two crosspieces.

She measures the warp frame with a tape measure to ensure that the crosspieces are even before taking the warp thread and wrapping it from one crosspiece to the other in a figure-eight pattern. Back and forth, Hazel wraps the yarn. Over and under, she moves the threads in a smooth rhythm. This figure-eight motion creates two sheds, which are actually two sets of warp threads separated by the alternating pattern. She passes a piece of string through the sheds as a marker and laces the warp to wooden dowels, anchoring it firmly to the loom.

Hazel now sits down to weave. She picks up the cross-yarn, called the weft, and feeds it through the

warp sheds. In and out, she weaves the yarn and packs it down with a weaving comb. Her fingers work quickly. At one point, she stops and tells us, "I like to build the yarn and make rugs. I use these weaving combs to beat down the yarns. My old man, who died a few years ago, made this comb for me. It is ironwood and is very hard." Hazel resumes her motion, and all is quiet except for the snap of the warp threads and the thumping of the comb against the yarn. After a few hours, she has woven several inches of the black border of the rug. "Now it is starting to look like something," she says.

She spends most of her daylight hours weaving, and by the end of three weeks, the rug is nearly finished. With only three more inches to go, it hangs on the loom. Her storm pattern is intricate. Its blacks, grays, and browns contrast beautifully with the reds and whites. Like most Navajo weavers, Hazel keeps the designs in her mind, weaving the inner patterns according to her own expectations.

Hazel is anxious to finish the storm pattern rug so she asks a neighbor to help. She explains, "The end is the hardest part. The strings are so tight." The neighbor wraps the yarn loosely around a thin stick and passes it through the warp strings. Hazel pulls the yarn through a small section of threads with her finger. She remarks,

"My sticks are all slicky. The lanolin from the wool makes them that way. I use all different sizes of sticks to feed the yarn. The smallest are for the ends." Soon the warp strings are so tight that she can no longer fit the stick into the sheds. "It's time to use my needle," she states. She now uses a table fork, instead of a comb, to press the yarn down. "The forks are smaller and help me push down the wool very, very hard. My aunt taught me about the fork. It works well when the amount to weave gets small."

The hours pass, the neighbor leaves, and Hazel continues to work at the loom. As evening approaches, the weaving shed grows cool. She stops only to light her lantern and build a fire. A soft glow fills the room and all is quiet except for the crackling of the fire. Although it seems that there is not a bit of space left to weave, Hazel adds additional yarn to the rug. She says, "You know, you sew it up until the threads don't show. You can't cheat and leave a hole." Over and over, Hazel continues to squeeze the yarn through the minute space. She starts to laugh. "I sometimes don't eat anything all day long. I just sit and weave. I put my hands on magic automatic!" At last, all the spaces are filled, and with a broad smile, Hazel says, "It is done. The dance with my hands is over." She sits back to admire her rug.

Hazel stands up, stretches, and removes the rug from the loom. Using a knife, she cuts the strings from the warp beams and with short tugs pulls them out. Next, she goes outside and shakes the rug, in the moonlight, to remove any dust. Inside the house, Hazel lays the rug across her bed, takes out a wire brush, and runs it quickly over the finished work. This brisk movement makes the surface of the yarn smooth. After a few minutes, she stops and holds up her creation. Hazel's voice and posture show signs of weariness, but she is proud of a job well done. "I'm worn out! I'm glad this is done," she sighs. "I'll sleep tonight."

Soil is from our
Earth Mother.
She is our
womb, and she
nourishes us and
encircles us with
her warmth.

Steven A. Darden

POTTERY

Mary Joe Yazzie and her mother-in-law, Annette, are well-known potters from Cow Springs, Arizona. "We have been making pots since we were really small. Our grandmas, aunts, mothers, and everybody taught us," explains Annette. The women call their pottery "earthpots" because all the materials used—clay, sap, and cinders—come from Annette's land.

On this warm and breezy day, we go to the clay pits not far from Annette's hogan. Waving her hands over a twenty-foot-wide parcel, Annette says, "I have been coming to this pit for clay since I was young." On this site consisting of rocks, sand, and clay, with a few sprawling juniper trees, the women take their shovels and jab them into the earth; their blades clang against rock. The monotonous rhythm of their work takes over, but soon the women create a gray landslide, breaking loose large chunks of clay. After the dust settles, they pace through the mounds and pick out several good pieces. Mary Joe tosses a few clumps into her bucket and says, "We look for only the best." "You don't want any sand in your clay," Annette adds. "Sometimes I bang two clay stones together to shake out the sand. The clay must be hard like a rock."

The women dig, pick, and choose carefully until their buckets are full. "This is hard work. I am all sweaty," says Mary Joe. "After we get back to camp, we will soak the clay overnight in a bucket of water to make it soft and easy to handle."

Next, we travel to a nearby forested area to collect pitch from the piñon trees. The sticky pitch, another essential ingredient for making pottery, is used as a sealing glaze. The piñon needles shine in the bright sunlight. Mary Joe points to brown, sticky pitch oozing from joints of the piñon branches. She picks up a stick in one hand, scrapes pitch from the bark of a tree, and plops it into a coffee can. She is pleased to find so much. "You see how sticky it is. It's like chewing gum. When we would herd sheep and were hungry, we would chew it like spearmint." As Mary Joe gathers more pitch, she says, "If you don't have enough, then your pot won't get shiny, so let's make sure the can is full."

Mary Joe moves from tree to tree, examining the branches. She says, "You know, when I was little, we used to take a picnic lunch when we went to find gum for making potteries. We used the gum for lots of other things, too. We put it on sores. We mixed it with Vaseline so the sores would heal. Also, you can put it on your face for sunburn or windburn. These old people don't run to the hospital. It's too far. They just use the gum."

After scraping the pitch from one last tree, Mary Joe is delighted. "I am lucky. Some days I walk and walk and find nothing. This is a good day." We return to Annette's hogan to rest and have a dinner of fry bread and stew.

The next morning, we drive to Annette's house with the cinder stones and firewood that Helen and I had agreed to contribute. After picking up a handful of the red lava cinders, Mary Joe smiles as she spreads them across a metate and says, "I call these stones 'ash,' and I'm going to grind them until they are very, very fine. Then I'll add them to the clay to help the pot become strong, stiff, and stand up right." She moves the grinding stones back and forth across the lava cinders on the metate. They make a loud scraping sound, but in a short time, she has turned the cinders into a fine red powder.

Using the bé'éžó, Mary Joe sweeps the ground ash from the metate onto a section of screen. "This acts as my sieve," she says. As she gently shakes the screen, the powdered ash falls through into a bucket. "You have to make sure there is no wood, sand, or hair in the ground ash. It has to be pure. If that stuff gets in there, then the pot will go wrong. You want everything to be clean. The half-cup of red ash is ready. Now we need the clay."

Mary Joe brings the bucket from the hogan. She lifts the mass of soaking clay from the water, dumps out the excess, and returns the clay to the bucket. Its wet, shiny surface bears no resemblance to the dusty gray rock that she dumped into the water on the previous day. She continues with the next step.

"After you grind the ash stones really fine, you mix it with clay. You make a good dough. The ash must be fine. If it is not, then the clay won't get smooth. You'll have lumps and bumps in the pots. Now, I'll mix the ash and clay until I have the good dough." The gallon of gray clay is soft and easy to mold. From the bucket, she takes a handful of clay, squeezes it, and adds a little of the lava ash. Again, she reaches into the clay bucket for another handful. Gradually, she increases the mass, kneading all the clay and powder cinders until they are completely mixed.

The mixture is now ready to form and shape. Mary Joe says, "Making the pot is the easy part to do." First, she takes two large handfuls of clay. "You kind of make this bottom piece into a piecrust so you are ready to shape the rest of the pot on it. You begin by taking another pottery that is already made, and you put it in the center of the clay piecrust." She places an old pot on the new base, which is about half-an-inch thick. With both hands, Mary Joe presses the dough around the pot using slow, careful fingertip movements to smooth the clay. She takes more clay and rolls it into a long rope. "I make these snake coils and wrap them around the top of the clay base. You keep making more and more strings and you keep wrapping them around until you have built the side of a high pot. Then you smooth it around a little bit. You remove the old pot from inside the new pot, and you smooth it more and more." With damp hands, Mary Joe rubs out the ridge coils.

Annette hands her a smooth old corncob, which she uses to pack the clay. "When you are working with the corncob, you can even put designs on the pots. You can add more clay and blend it or make grooves in it. The corncob is a good tool to use in making pots." She swishes the cob around the pot, both inside and out, until the clay is compressed to half its original thickness. Mary Joe pauses and admires her new creation. The base is full and round and its top is tall and straight. "This will be a beautiful pottery when it is finished."

The next step in making pottery is the drying process. "You have to let the pot dry completely. That is very, very important. If you are in a hurry, you can let it dry by the stove for about eight hours. If the clay is thick on the pot, then it will take a few days. If the pots are not dried thoroughly, then they won't cook right. The first time I made a pot, it didn't dry. I just couldn't wait. I was so excited, I wanted to see it cooked. I didn't let it dry enough. I cooked it, and it cracked and popped! We are not in a hurry, so we will let this pot dry for a few days, then we know we are safe." Mary Joe enters Annette's hogan, looks for a protected place, and chooses a spot on the highest shelf. She says, "I'll put this pot up really high so the babies won't get to it and knock it down and break it."

Five days later, we meet back at the camp. Mary Joe says, "Now let's check for dryness." Her fingers slide over the clay surface. "It's ready," she judges. "It's good and dry. Now we can fire it." Mary Joe tells Annette and Gail, Annette's married daughter, to begin building a fire. Gail swings her ax, chopping juniper into small bits. With this kindling and a few large logs, she builds a hot, crackling fire. Mary Joe carefully places the pot on the ground a few inches from the flames. "I'm going to heat it slowly." She leans the pot on its side for fifteen minutes before turning it with a stick. The fire soon burns down to smoldering coals, and the pot is ready to be cooked. Mary Joe uses two sticks to turn the pot so its mouth faces the flames; she spreads the coals and works them around it. Quickly, she adds more kindling to the fire, covering the coals and pot. "See," she says as the blaze swirls around the wood, "you can't even tell that a pot is in the fire."

Mary Joe turns to Gail. It is time to melt the pitch. Gail places the can of pitch close to the fire as Mary Joe explains, "I put the gum here by the heat because it needs to melt." Before long, the pitch liquifies and begins to boil.

As the piñon pitch melts and the pot fires, Gail tells us that different kinds of wood affect the color of the pottery. "Juniper can give you a tan or gray color, and the piñon wood can give you a white color. The oak makes the pot a dark brown. Sometimes you just don't know. It can always be a surprise. Also, you can change the wood in the middle of cooking and get different colors."

The fire burns down, so Mary Joe takes a stick and slowly works the pot away from the ashes. Next, she rubs the ashes off her pot with a paper bag. Using two sticks, she lifts the pot and places it on a board. While it cools, Mary Joe checks the boiling pitch. "It is just right. Now we are ready to put the pitch on the pottery."

As she scoops up pitch with a stick and dabs it lightly on the pot, it begins to sizzle and smoke. "Oops!" she says. "The pot is just a little too hot. It is not ready for the gum. You want to let it cool just the right amount of time because if you put the gum on too soon, the heat of the pot will burn the sap black. If you wait a few minutes, then the pot will cool a little and you can put the gum on. Then it will show the color made from the kind of wood you chose. Any pot can be black. You want to work for a different color."

She tests the pot once more and says, "Okay. We are ready." With a glob of pitch at the end of her stick, Mary Joe quickly rubs it all over the pot, inside and out. The dry, hot clay absorbs the pitch quickly and begins to turn a rich, dark red. She picks up more gum with her stick and rubs down the inside, gently stirring the pot as fragrant smoke rises in the air.

When it has cooled, she rubs the pottery with a piece of waxed paper. "In the old days, we used piñon boughs to shine our pots." She polishes the pot and the glaze shines brightly.

Mary Joe is proud of her pot as she holds it up to the sun. "We Navajos use our pottery. You can boil water in these pots. In the old days, this is all we used." With a smile on her face, Mary Joe adds, "I love to be with things in the traditional way. When I was little and we did things in the old way, I would watch and watch —and remember."

MUD OVEN

Helen and I are curious about traditional mud ovens, and through Yazzie, who showed us how to build a summer shelter, we learn that his mother frequently uses one. Yazzie introduces us and acts as translator.

Addie Yazzie uses her outdoor mud oven to cook corn, bread, and meat. "I make some pretty good food in my oven. These meats come out juicy, and the corns and bread are soft and moist.

"My oven comes straight from the earth." Water, soil, and rock are used to build it, and, if built correctly, one can last as long as twenty years. "My husband made my oven for me a long time ago. When you make such an oven, you have to do a good job and take your time."

Addie, through Yazzie, continues: "First , you pick a spot on the ground and make it nice. Pick out the weeds and rocks. Rub water over the place so it is flat and smooth. Then find lots of big rocks. These rocks are a special kind. They can take lots of hot heat. I call them 'the rocks that don't explode in the fire.' After you collect about fifteen or twenty big rocks, put them in a circle, a circle about three feet around, but make sure you leave an opening for a door that faces east because all our door openings face that way. Pile the rocks really tall until you have a nice wall about three feet high. Next, lay a big flat rock across the top of the walls. That's the roof of the oven. We find another flat rock for the door. This oven sort of has the shape of a baby hogan."

After the walls are standing, mud plaster is applied to the rocks. "We mix water and lots of dirt together to make the covering for the oven. We call this 'Navajo cement.' With a flat shovel, we scoop up the mud and throw it on the rocks. We cover all the rocks, including the door, with the cement. The mud is about two or three inches thick. We let the mud dry so it is hard, and next we rub it down with water to make it smooth. By then, you have a pretty good oven, and it is all ready to go."

Addie's oven is twenty yards from her hogan. The beehive-shaped mud dome blends well with the landscape, making it difficult to locate amidst the dust piles and brown autumn fields.

"Sometimes after it rains, some of the mud washes off, so we have to make up more plaster to cover the holes. It's easy to do, and it keeps the oven in pretty good working order."

With a smile Addie adds, "This oven is a good thing to have. We can bake good foods. They taste good cooked on cedar and piñon coals. I kind of feel like I cook in the earth."

THE HOGAN

The hogan is an integral part of the Navajos' connection to the land; it represents a piece of personal property and consists of natural elements such as stone, wood, or mud. Unfortunately, structures such as these are also caught up in the Hopi-Navajo Land Dispute. Ella Deal tells us of one such case: "Delbert Begay could not finish his hogan for his mother. He started it last year and was told he could not finish it." This half-finished hogan is an interesting structure to examine in terms of construction.

The skeleton of the hogan stands in a field of sage. Delbert's twenty-year-old son, Darrel, a college student, is home visiting the Begay camp. He gives us a tour of the camp: a two-room house, a shed, and this partially built hogan, where six juniper posts remain upright and only part of the roof has been woven. The remaining logs and piles of mud clutter the base of the unfinished hogan.

We move into the empty space, each choosing a ground log to sit on. Without prompting, Darrel speaks. "This hogan is to be for my grandma. She is wanting a place of her own because our other house is getting too crowded. So we started to build this one for her and the government man tells us to stop. It's hard living knowing you can't be with your land."

We are quiet before Darrel begins to speak again.

"My dad and I started this hogan a couple of years ago. To build a hogan, you have to clear the land to make it flat." He motions to the floor of his grandmother's hogan. "Then we get together all of the wood we need to build the hogan. We cut our logs in a forest not too far from here and bring them back to the camp. We have to start getting pretty picky when we choose the logs. We take only the big, fat cedar [juniper] for our walls. Once we get only the good wood, we trim them and make them square on the ends and sides, like the wall log you are sitting on. Before we build, we always check to make sure we have enough logs for the roof and walls.

"You use what is on your land. If you have lots of mud, you make a mud hogan. If you live close to rocks, you have a stone one, and if you live close to logs, then you have a wood one. Most of the time, people will use a mixture of rock, log, and mud. Our land has a little bit of everything.

"After the logs are readied, we put six posts in a circle. We make sure that the posts are about five to six feet apart. I usually walk about five or six steps to mark a spot for each post, then we put stringer posts between the six standing ones. This is the start of the roof.

"To make the roof, we take logs with different lengths. We measure this wood with a rope to make

sure each log is the right size. My cousins and uncles help with the roof. We pick up the logs and hand them to the roof-makers. Only the men with lots of experience must do the roof. You don't want the ceiling too low or too high. Too much weight can make the log walls crack, and too many logs make the roof too heavy. We lay the logs across each other, making a circle that looks like an upside-down basket. This is as far as we got on my grandma's hogan before we were told to stop building. That sure was a hard time for us. . . .

"This making a hogan can take pretty long unless you have a lot of help. Sometimes our family and neighbors come to help out, then the building goes pretty fast.

"After the roof, we do the walls. We use fat cedar and cut the ends so they will fit the main posts. We build the logs around the posts so they fit one on top of the other. We don't worry about the holes in the walls. We can always patch them up with wood chips, juniper bark, or rags and cover them with mud. I like to make the walls as tall as I am. The wall facing east is always shorter. This makes room for the door hole. Our doors face east so we can say hello to the sun. We trim up the doorway and make it neat. We get a wooden door to put over the opening. Some people in the old days used a buckskin or rug to cover the door hole.

"Next, we close up the hogan nice and tight. Once the holes are filled, we cover the roof with juniper bark. We call this 'Navajo tar paper.' We take these wide strips and lay them across the top, and then we pile on wood chips. We shovel them up really high so they reach the rooftop.

"Then we put on the finishing touches. We have to cook the dirt and put it between the cracks in the walls, and we cover the roof with it, too. First, we make a big fire, and we take a big washtub, fill it with water, and put it on the fire to boil. When the water is pretty hot, we add the dirt and stir it into mud. I guess you could also call this plaster.

"You take this mud and you stand about a foot from the walls, and you throw the mud into the cracks. Then you rub the mud in with your fingers so it becomes smooth and even. It also gets kind of messy.

"After we do the walls, then we do the roof. We use only the best heavy dirt and mud. We throw the mud up high and cover the roof. It takes long, and we have to do it right. If you don't, you have problems. When it snows, we might have a surprise in the morning of water dripping on our heads. When this happens, we have to redo the clay, cover the holes, and fix it right. Sometimes we even put down plastic in bad weather. We hold it down with rocks, which keeps the roof dry and us dry.

"We take oil drums and cut them in half to be a stove. If you look up in this hogan, you will see a hole left. We would have run a pipe from the stove up high to the hole. That is our chimney. The oil drum is a cook stove and a fireplace.

"Once we put in the oil drum, we are pretty much ready to move in. We check the walls and the roof to make sure everything is tight, then we can move in our furniture: a couple of beds, a chest of drawers, shelves, clothes, kitchen stuff. It feels good to move into your new home."

The hogan is important to the Navajos for material reasons, but also has significant religious meaning. The first hogan was included in the Navajo creation story: First Man and First Woman asked the Holy People to build a hogan made of white shell and abalone. Traditionally, the doorway of all hogans faces east to greet the morning sun of father sky. The inside of the hogan is a symbolic representation of mother earth's womb. These beliefs have been passed down through the generations, and the wood, rock, and mud continue to encircle the Navajos in a protective manner.

△△△△

LIST OF PLATES